POLICE AT WORK

Perspectives in Criminal Justice 5

ABOUT THE SERIES

The Perspectives in Criminal Justice Series is designed to meet the research information needs of faculty, students and professionals who are studying and working in the field fo criminal justice. The *Series* will cover a wide variety of research approaches and issues related to criminal justice. The books are collections of articles not previously published, and each book will focus on specific themes, research topics, or controversial issues.

The articles selected for publication are revised versions of papers presented at the annual meetings of the Academy of Criminal Justice Sciences. Papers organized around a specific topic are reviewed by the book's editor and a panel or referees for comment and suggestions for revision. The *Series* will rely on a multidisciplinary approach to such topical areas as organizational theory and change, the nature of crime, law and social control, and applied research as well as the traditional areas of police, courts, corrections, and juvenile justice.

The current volumes include:

- *Corrections at the Crossroads: Designing Policy*, edited by Sherwood E. Zimmerman and Harold D. Miller
- *Race, Crime and Criminal Justice*, edited by R. L. McNeely and Carl E. Pope
- *Coping with Imprisonment*, edited by Nicolette Parisi
- *Managing Police Work: Issues and Analysis*, edited by Jack R. Greene
- *Police at Work: Policy Issues and Analysis*, edited by Richard R. Bennett

Comments and suggestions from our readers are encouraged and welcomed.

Series Editor
John A. Conley
Criminal Justice Program
University of Wisconsin—Milwaukee

Perspectives in Criminal Justice 5

Police at Work
Policy Issues and Analysis

Edited by
Richard R. Bennett

*Published in cooperation with
the Academy of Criminal Justice Sciences*

SAGE PUBLICATIONS
Beverly Hills / London / New Delhi

For information address:

SAGE Publications, Inc.
275 South Beverly Drive
Beverly Hills, California 90212

SAGE Publications India Pvt. Ltd.      SAGE Publications Ltd
    C-236 Defence Colony   28 Banner Street
    New Delhi 110 024, India   London EC1Y 8QE, England

Printed in the United States of America

Library of Congress Cataloging in Publication Data

Main entry under title:

Police at Work.

    (Perspectives in criminal justice ; 5)
    "Published in cooperation with the Academy of
Criminal Justice Sciences."
    Bibliography: p.
    1. Police—United States—Addresses, essays, lec-
tures.   2. Police—Government policy—United States—
Addresses, essays, lectures.   3. Work environment—
United States—Addresses, essays, lectures.   I. Bennett,
Richard R.   II. Academy of Criminal Justice Sciences.
III.   Series.

HV8138.P665   1983   363.2'3'0973   82-23126
ISBN 0-8039-1956-5
ISBN 0-8039-1957-3 (pbk.)

FIRST PRINTING

CONTENTS

INTRODUCTION:
Police Policy Research in the 1980s

Richard R. Bennett

The American University

Unlike the birth of Athena from the head of Zeus, the direction and content of police policy research has evolved over time, receiving impetus from the political environment while being guided by social and economic events. Two political and economic factors in particular have played important roles in the development of police policy research for the 1980s. Politically, there has been a shift in the last twenty years from a liberal, social conscience orientation to a conservative approach valuing maintenance of the status quo. At the same time, there has been a not-so-subtle shift in governmental funding from areas of social concern to economic problems and national defense. The effects of these shifts have been exacerbated by an overall decline in the fiscal robustness of the nation's economy.

The impact of these two trends has brought about a shift in public policy concerning crime from a focus on its etiology and amelioration through the manipulation of social conditions to a focus on the control of crime through a strengthening of the justice system, especially the role of the police. There has also been a discernible change in police policy for controlling crime over the last decade. Policy concerns have moved from considerations at the macro level of the police function and organization, through intermediate levels such as police procedures, to the micro level of

Author's Note: *The author would like to thank James J. Fyfe, The American University, and Sandra Baxter, Advanced Technology, Inc., for their comments and aid in completing this introduction.*

analysis and the police working environment. A discussion of the historical contexts of these shifts helps in understanding the research agenda of scholars studying police policy issues today.

FROM CRIME CAUSATION TO CRIME CONTROL

World War II devastated the industrial capacities of Europe and Japan. The United States emerged from the conflict with its huge industrial complex intact and growing. The subsequent rebuilding of the world's economy placed the United States in a most favorable position. It became the world's supplier of reconstruction machinery and technology, and as a result the nation entered a period of escalating prosperity. The unprecedented economic growth and the isolationist policies of the Eisenhower years fostered an introspective atmosphere and interest in internal social problems such as crime.

Two other factors contributed to the emergence of crime as a "new" social problem in the 1950s. As children born in the postwar baby boom aged, their sheer number brought attention to problems of juvenile delinquency. Second, and more important, the war years and the industrial boom of the postwar period changed the demographic and social characteristics of the nation's urban areas. Large migrations of unskilled southern blacks changed the social landscape of the north. Their numbers and their difficulties in assimilating to an industrialized job market spawned conflict and crime. These two demographic shifts coincided with postwar optimism that American ingenuity could solve any problem and led to theorizing about the "roots of crime" and to the implementation of programs attempting to eliminate these roots.

The 1950s and 1960s saw the emergence of a plethora of crime causation theories which focused on the conditions of urban life. Cohen (1955), Merton (1957), Miller (1958), and Cloward and Ohlin (1960), to name but a few, offered theories that became the bases of governmental efforts to ameliorate the social conditions that spawned criminality. Policies derived from these theoretical perspectives were implemented in the 1960s in large-scale social change projects. The Mobilization for Youth was one action program that attempted to eliminate the "roots" of crime by giving opportunities, such as job training and employment, to disadvantaged youths (Helfgot, 1974).

Government-funded efforts to eliminate crime at its roots were short-lived, however. The action programs implemented during the early 1960s did not demonstrate the expected positive effects, and urban crime went unchecked. Researchers as well as policymakers began to see that in their zeal to implement programs, they had not carefully analyzed the basic problems. They realized that crime was a more complex social phenomenon than they had thought and that a few "quick-fix action programs" or the simple infusion of money into problem areas had small chances of success. These misgivings became formal conclusions with the 1965 outbreak of urban riots in Watts and other cities. The failure of efforts to control crime through social action and the eruption of mass urban disorder signaled the end of America's flirtation with policies focused on crime causation.

The government, in response to citizens' perceptions of lawlessness, shifted their policy from an emphasis on crime causation to an emphasis on control. The shift to control was quickened in the late 1960s by the proliferation of antiwar demonstrations, which presented a new set of "criminal behaviors" necessitating control. Thus, as the Johnson presidential years came to a close, the concept and programs of the Great Society lost political favor and a law and order mentality began to sweep the nation. The new orientation reflected the conclusion that solving crime was a utopian dream but controlling crime appeared to be a realistic goal. Gallup and Harris public opinion polls conducted in the mid- and late 1960s documented a shift in priority concerns from housing and employment to crime (Bennett, 1975).

President Johnson responded to this public sentiment by creating the Office of Law Enforcement Assistance (in 1965), later to be called the Law Enforcement Assistance Administration (in 1968). Johnson also convened commissions to study crime and crime prevention. The first was the President's Commission on Law Enforcement and the Administration of Justice, also known as the President's Crime Commission (1965). Its name alone signaled the change in policy focus. Although its 1967 report did include discussion of crime causation, it heavily emphasized the effects of the criminal justice system, and especially the police, on crime control. Other commissions concerned with problems of disorder and crime were established in the late 1960s in response to public awareness of crime. The National Advisory Commission on Civil Disorders (1967) and the National Commission on the Causes and Prevention of Violence (1968) continued to emphasize control.

The crime control policy orientation reached its nadir in the 1968 presidential election. Candidate Nixon declared a war on crime and stressed his law and order platform. He won the election by capitalizing on both the public's fear of urban lawlessness and Vice President Humphrey's symbolic attachment to Johnson's failed war policies.

Once in office, Nixon formally launched his war on crime and the "Law and Order Movement" was born (see Bennett, 1975, for a more detailed discussion). He began funneling money into the Law Enforcement Assistance Administration and the criminal justice establishment generally. Public expenditures for armaments, communications equipment, and crime control devices and technology reached unprecedented levels. This mentality also pervaded the private crime control sector. Expenditures for private security and personal protection devices also escalated sharply.

Academics and crime theoreticians reflected this new crime control mentality by subtly changing their emphases from the correlates of crime such as poverty, social deterioration, and blocked legitimate and illegitimate means to theories of crime based on the mechanisms of power and the operations of the criminal justice system. Theories no longer concerned causal social conditions but instead sought to explain how the political environment defined crime and how the criminal justice system generated criminals. This theorizing took two paths. First, conflict theorists such as Quinney (1970) and Turk (1969) detailed how the political system defined criminality and how the police created crime. Second, labeling theorists discussed how the operation of the justice system continued criminality (Lemert, 1972; Schur, 1971).

The late 1960s, then, signaled a change in policy from one of causation to one of control. The large amounts of money once spent to rectify crime-producing social conditions evaporated, and shrinking finances and the raging recession forced policymakers to redirect their efforts to less costly and more politically visible crime control tactics. Once control was viewed as the sine qua non of countercrime activities, the justice establishment was seen as the natural focus of policy efforts. Since police were seen as the front line of the justice establishment's war on crime, implementation of crime control policies logically fell to the police.

POLICE POLICY RESEARCH AND ANALYSIS: THE LATE 1960s AND THE DECADE OF THE 1970s

Policy shifts concerning control of crime and the police in the late 1960s and throughout the 1970s can best be understood by employing a scope perspective: policy moved from the macro level of analysis to the micro level. It was first believed that effective crime control could be accomplished through optimal organization and administration of the police agency. The vast majority of the policy research and analysis during this time focused on increasing the organization's ability to institute control.

Indicative of this emphasis was the Ford Foundation's establishment of the Police Foundation in 1970. Funded with $30 million dollars over a five-year period, the Police Foundation was charged to provide police management training, education programs, and even a national police college. The rationale behind such programs was simple: enable police agencies to upgrade their management and subsequently improve the crime control services they provide. In short, the policy answer to the perceived lawlessness was to strengthen police agencies by renovating their organizational structure, enlarging their supply of hardware, and increasing the managerial competence of administrative officers.

The grants and contracts let by the then National Institute of Law Enforcement and Criminal Justice (a division of LEAA) in this period also reflected the control orientation. Of the 57 projects funded between 1969 and 1970 (excluding 16 projects in forensic science), 42 percent dealt with macro-level issues of the police role and organization and their relations to crime and the community (National Institute of Justice, 1982). In a similar vein, researchers such as Bittner (1970) and commissions such as the President's Commission on Law Enforcement and the Administration of Justice (1967) and the National Advisory Commission on Criminal Justice Standards and Goals convened in 1971 were raising the same questions. Books like the revised *Municipal Police Administration* (Eastman and Eastman, 1969) began appearing. In short, the general policy tone of the late 1960s and the early 1970s highlighted the activities and administration of the police because crime control was construed as an organizational problem.

As the mid-1970s approached, the ineffectiveness of policy focusing on police organization became apparent. Crime continued to increase regardless of efforts to improve agency administration and resources (Goldstein, 1977). Policymakers then shifted their focus from the macro level to an intermediate level of analysis and emphasized agency procedures. This shift was made for two reasons. First, policies based on restructuring police agencies had not counteracted growing crime rates. Second, although the structural approach might promise results in the long run, the public demanded more immediate solutions.

The National Institute of Law Enforcement and Criminal Justice reflected, and reinforced, this shift to a more intermediate level of police agency functioning in their funding decisions. Of the 76 proposals funded between 1971 and 1976, 40 percent of the nonforensic science projects studied police procedures directed toward control of criminality (National Institute of Justice, 1982). Examples of funded projects include Budnick's examination of intensive police patrol funded in 1971, Greenwood's analysis of the criminal investigation process funded in 1974, the Kansas City Police Department's response time analysis study funded in 1974, the National Sheriffs' Association's evaluation of team policing funded in 1975, Schell's evaluation of traditional preventive patrol funded in 1975, and Greenberg's felony investigation decision model, also funded in 1975.

The new focus guided privately funded research as well. The Police Foundation, which by this time had changed its mission, conducted extensive projects on police procedures during this period. The *Kansas City Preventive Patrol Project* (Kelling et al., 1974), the *San Diego Field Interrogation Experiment* (Boydstun, 1975), *Managing Investigations: The Rochester System* (Bloch and Bell, 1976), and *The Cincinnati Team Policing Experiment* (Schwartz and Clarren, 1977) were projects funded by and in most cases conducted by the Foundation.

The results of this research and policy analysis were just as, if not more, disappointing than those conducted on the organizational level. Finding after finding indicated that policy implemented on the intermediate level of agency procedures was not producing the desired reduction in crime. Policymakers began to look closer at the functioning of police officers themselves. They believed that if agency programs and procedures were ineffectual, the fault might lie at the micro level with the quality, motivation, and performance of officers.

This change in focus to the police working environment was due not only to the lack of significant success in policy research on the intermediate or procedural level, but also to the changing and deteriorating economic conditions of the nation. Whereas the late 1960s and early 1970s saw a dwindling economy due to foreign competition and the war in Vietnam, the mid-1970s saw an economic downturn due to the oil embargo and impending recession. For the first time in ten years, the war on crime took second place to citizens' concerns about employment, inflation, and the economy. In response, federal research money for crime control began to disappear and large-scale research projects on the crime problem became rare. Research then focused on the micro level and, not coincidentally, on crime control policies that would be not too costly to implement.

The micro-level issues included ways to increase longevity of police employment, measures to reduce per-person costs of recruitment and training, efforts to lessen police stress and ineffective officer behaviors, and better measurement of police actions generally. The projects funded by the National Institute of Justice reflected, and reinforced, the new policy orientation. From 1977 to 1980, NIJ funded 45 nonforensic projects of which 36 percent dealt with issues of the police work environment, such as performance, stress, labor relations, and officer discretion. Private research organizations followed suit, as evidenced by the Police Foundation's publication of the *Dallas Experience: Human Resources* (Kelling and Wycoff, 1978). Professional journal articles and conference presentations over the last four years have discussed a significant number of research projects concerning the effects of stress, officer selection and attrition, and especially performance evaluation.

In summary, during the last twelve years, police policy research has linearly moved from a focus on the organizational or macro level to the micro level of police working environment. The changes have been due to factors in the political and economic sectors, reductions in funding for costly experimental programs, and research findings indicating that organizational and then procedural policy foci had not reduced crime.

POLICY RESEARCH IN THE 1980s

With unemployment rising to double-digit levels, a national budget with a record-breaking deficit, and foreign competition closing the doors of our once powerful manufacturing complex, costly crime control efforts have been under close scrutiny in the early 1980s. Evidence continues to mount that the justice system and especially the police have failed in their mission to curb crime and control lawlessness. These factors have again generated a new set of policy agendas. Policy analysts have begun asking the important and difficult question obscured in the 1970s rush to find effective police programs: What is the actual province of the police, and what impact can the police realistically expect to have on the prevention and control of crime? Further, policy analysts have accepted the reality that large-scale social spending programs and massive infusion of funds to the police are no longer feasible. The question is what less costly efforts might prove effective?

Policy research in the 1980s will focus on two different but complementary topics. First, what is the role of the police in crime prevention and control? Second, how can the police working environment be modified to optimize the delivery of police services? The first issue is whether the police actually control crime or whether their real function is to offer the community other crime-related services, such as the maintenance of order and the generation of a sense of community well-being (Wilson and Kelling 1982). Similarly, should the police attempt to control all crime or should they more realistically limit their attention to certain categories of crimes and criminals (Petersilia, 1980)? The National Institute of Justice funded a project in 1982 to investigate the order maintenance function of the police, as opposed to their law enforcement function. There has also been renewed interest in the community and its ability to control criminal behavior. Projects designed to mobilize communities to fight crime through citizen action have been proliferating. As an example, the Department of Housing and Urban Development recently funded a community anticrime evaluation project for public housing. In a similar vein, local police departments have recently become involved in organizing community block groups and neighborhood crime watch programs.

The second policy focus of the 1980s, and the focus of this book, is on the police working environment. The drive to improve police officer performance in the area of community crime-related services will necessitate policy research into issues such as attrition and the retention of the most qualified officers, as well as research investigating police stress and its effects on performance. Next, the entire issue of police performance will become a major research and policy topic. Issues such as effectiveness and ineffectiveness of police behavior in delivering crime related services, the actual measurement of such performance, and, subsequently, the distribution of departmental rewards for performance will become more pressing as the economy further declines and the need for community crime-related services concomitantly increases. Finally, the delivery of police services will attract more attention as a topic in the 1980s. More and more concern will focus on how police services are delivered, and especially how the organization determines what services are to be performed, in what order of importance, at what speed, and who within the police establishment will have the discretion to make that determination.

OVERVIEW OF THE VOLUME

In response to the economic and political events occurring over the past twenty years, a policy and analysis agenda has evolved for police research in the 1980s. This book presents research and policy analysis on the cutting edge of this agenda. Each of the seven chapters reports research focusing on the police working environment. The police working environment is defined as that constellation of structures and processes that determine, at an operational level, the extent and quality of police service delivery. Thus, the investigation of the police working environment focuses upon the police officers themselves and their relationship to the job, the organization, and the community they serve.

The selections included in this volume relate to this emerging policy agenda in two significant ways. First, they focus on the nature of police service from the perspective of the workers and their ability to perform, rather than on the effects of their performance. Given this perspective, the impact of job stress and its resultant effect on attrition take on a new and important meaning in understanding job quality and performance competence. Likewise, performance measurement and the analysis of the reward structure become crucial topics in policy research aimed at upgrading police services to the community.

Second, the research presented in this volume addresses the police working environment as it affects the delivery of crime-related services. These studies differ from those conducted in the 1970s in significant ways. The issue in the 1980s is not whether a certain departmental procedure affects crime, but how the structure and process of police work highlight certain services, imply a priority ranking of services, and determine the speed of service delivery to the community. In addition, these studies investigate the conceptual bases of service determination. In short, the studies presented in this volume address a critical emerging policy area, the police working environment.

REFERENCES

BENNETT, R. R. (1975) "Crime and Law," in A. L. Mauss (ed.) Social Problems as Social Movements. Philadelphia: Lippincott.
BITTNER, E. (1970) The Functions of the Police in Modern Society. Washington, DC: U.S. Government Printing Office.
BLOCH, P. and J. BELL (1976) Managing Investigations: The Rochester System. Washington, DC: Police Foundation.
BOYDSTUN, J. (1975) San Diego Field Interrogation Experiment: Final Report. Washington, DC: Police Foundation.
CLOWARD, R. A. and L. E. OHLIN (1960) Delinquency and Opportunity: A Theory of Delinquent Gangs. New York: Free Press.
COHEN, A. (1955) Delinquent Boys. New York: Free Press.

EASTMAN, G. and E. EASTMAN [eds.] (1969) Municipal Police Administration. Washington, DC: International City Managers Association.

GOLDSTEIN, H. (1977) Policing a Free Society. Cambridge, MA: Ballinger.

HELFGOT, J. (1974) "Professional reform organizations and the symbolic representation of the poor." American Sociological Review 39: 475-491.

KELLING, G. and A. WYCOFF (1978) The Dallas Experience: Human Resources Development. Washington, DC: Police Foundation.

KELLING, G. et al. (1974) The Kansas City Preventive Patrol Experiment. Washington, DC: Police Foundation.

LEMERT, E. M. (1972) Human Deviance, Social Problems, and Social Control. Englewood Cliffs, NJ: Prentice-Hall.

MERTON, R. K. (1957) Social Theory and Social Structure. New York: Free Press.

MILLER, W. (1958) "Lower class culture as a generating milieu of gang delinquency." Journal of Social Issues 14: 5-19.

National Institute of Justice (1982) Police Research Catalog. Washington, DC: U.S. Government Printing Office.

PETERSILIA, J. (1980) "Criminal career research: A review of recent evidence," in N. Morris and M. Tonry (eds.) Crime and Justice: An Annual Review of Research. Chicago: University of Chicago Press.

President's Commission on Law Enforcement and the Administration of Justice (1967) The Challenge of Crime in a Free Society. Washington, DC: U.S. Government Printing Office.

QUINNEY, R. (1970) The Social Reality of Crime. Boston: Little, Brown.

SCHUR, E. M. (1971) Labeling Deviant Behavior. New York: Harper & Row.

SCHWARTZ, A. I. and S. N. CLARREN (1977) The Cincinnati Team Policing Experiment. Washington, DC: Police Foundation.

TURK, A. (1969) Criminality and the Legal Order. Chicago: Rand McNally.

WILSON, J. Q. and G. KELLING (1982) "Broken windows." Atlantic Monthly (March): 29-38.

I.

Police Performance

The time-worn adage that "patrol is the backbone of the police agency" is taking on new meaning and policy ramifications in the 1980s. While the organizational reference of the phrase, that is, the delivery point of police services, remains accurate, the research on police patrol has shifted focus. Previously, studies on patrol have been descriptive and sought to analyze its functions; now, research is critically evaluating patrol performance. Since the working environment for the majority of sworn officers is the patrol, concern for effective police actions, criteria for patrol performance evaluation, and control and supervision of those actions are major issues in police work generally.

The three chapters contained in Part I deal specifically with these working environment topics. McIver and Parks present research and analysis focusing on performance in four traditional categories of police intervention. The purpose of their research is to identify police actions that are either effective or ineffective in dealing with police-citizen encounters. The authors note that earlier studies have focused on the categorization and explanation of police behavior rather than an evaluation of its effectiveness on citizen levels of satisfaction, attitudes toward the police, and the officer's ability to reduce emotional tension in the encounter. They argue that these indicators are more reflective of the police service mission than the traditional measures of arrest and conviction.

To accomplish their evaluative task, the authors observed over 1,600 police-citizen encounters involving 28 separate police behaviors. Through regression analysis they determined which actions were effective or ineffective in producing citizen satisfaction, positive attitudes, and a reduction of interactional tension. The findings indicate that there are, in fact, specific police actions that enhance the effectiveness of service delivery to the community. The policy implications of these findings are clear. Armed with this type of knowledge, policymakers can move to restructure the police service delivery system to maximize positive outcomes, can create and implement training to achieve this performance goal, and can reorganize the current reward structures to maintain their effects.

If services to the community are to be enhanced by more effective behavior, the officer's knowledge of the community and his or her ability to exercise good judgment must also be stressed as performance evaluation criteria. Mastrofski's work on alternative evaluation criteria addresses this important problem. He maintains that the knowledge and judgment required of an officer to deliver police services effectively is generated through close contact with citizens and citizen organizations. He further contends that performance evaluation based on arrests and convictions tends to direct officers' energies to these activities, to the detriment of developing a solid understanding of the community he or she serves. If service delivery to the community is an important function of police work, Mastrofski argues, performance evaluation must be expanded to include community knowledge. He investigated the relationship between six organizational arrangements and the officer's knowledge of the beat. He found that current and traditional arrangements have little effect on generating knowledge. He concludes that officer knowledge, and improvements in the delivery of community services, can be gained only through changes in agency organizational and performance evaluation.

Evaluation of police services to the community by line supervisors is the topic of the final chapter in Part I. This work rounds out the discussion of performance evaluation policy through its analysis of organizational control over patrol officer performance. If certain police behaviors and knowledge are known to be especially effective and responsive to the community, as argued in the first two chapters, the organization must have the ability to reward officers demonstrating them.

Allen and Maxfield maintain that supervisory control over patrol officers is problematic for two reasons. First, the police lack a clear public mandate about their role, which makes community-responsive evaluation difficult. Second, positive incentives to gain performance compliance are not formally available within the police establishment, and supervisors traditionally have relied on disincentives alone. The authors investigated the policy issue of supervisory control of performance by analyzing two models of control and reward, the command and bargaining models. They conclude, after analysis of supervisory expectations and patrol performance, that the bargaining model is the more promising in the effort to gain behavioral compliance of patrol officers.

Together, these three chapters illustrate the complex but important questions research and policy analysts must raise in order to understand and to modify the police working environment. It is through modifying the working environment that police services to the community can be enhanced and the effectiveness of the police increased.

1.

EVALUATING POLICE PERFORMANCE:
Identification of Effective and Ineffective Police Actions

John P. McIver
Roger B. Parks
Indiana University

Over the past two decades, our knowledge about the delivery of police services has grown by leaps and bounds. Unfortunately, we still cannot accurately predict the consequences of various decisions about how to produce policing, nor can we easily modify police practices in order to achieve desired levels and types of police services. The purpose of this report is to move us a step closer to the realization of these goals.

Crime has increased rapidly in recent years. So have other demands made on police agencies. Many jobs once considered not part of the law enforcement function have come to be recognized as important *police* duties regardless of whether or not they relate to law enforcement (Goldstein, 1977). Furthermore, in the wake of cutbacks in government services, police agencies have had even more responsibilities heaped upon them.

Thus we know police have several jobs to do. That they are not always successful in fulfilling their mission is also well known. We need to know not only what has to be done, but also how it should be done. Unless the police official or the government bureaucrat can acquire the latter information and can communicate it to the police serving the community, improvements in police service will be a function of luck or the unique abilities of certain "natural" police officers. It is our goal to try to provide some mechanism for judging police activities that will permit constructive assessment. We hope to improve the chances that changes can be made in the way police services are delivered to increase their value to the citizens receiving them.

POLICE EFFECTIVENESS:
THE LEGACY OF EMPIRICAL RESEARCH

Although patrol officers, as the on-the-street agents of their department, are the initial police representatives at almost all crime and non-crime incidents, their effectiveness as individual officers has been the subject of comparatively little research. With the few exceptions discussed below, the focus of research has been the department and not the officer. Failure to consider the effectiveness of the officer is due both to the difficulty in collecting data about the performance of particular officers and to the ease of gathering and analyzing department crime statistics.

A department's statistics are the consequences of all of the actions of of its officers. Very likely, there is more variation in officer effectiveness within a department than there is in mean effectiveness levels across departments. Highly effective officers work side by side with much less able patrolmen. This will be true of police officer performance in handling any of the myriad problems the public requests that they deal with. It is not necessarily true, however, that an officer can do as good a job in dealing with a domestic argument as he or she can in responding to a robbery. Officers are likely to be effective at certain tasks, but each officer will be better at some tasks than at others. Very few officers are likely to be able to handle with a high degree of success all the situations the police must face.

By and large, studies that have focused on the individual officers have not been concerned with officer effectiveness. Rather, most research on police officers in general, and patrol officers in particular, concentrates on cataloguing and explaining officer behavior. This conclusion describes almost all results published from observational studies, the method most appropriate for examining questions of officer performance. (See, for example, Black, 1970, 1980; Black and Reiss, 1970; Friedrich, 1980; Sykes and Clark, 1975; Wilson, 1968; Reiss, 1971; Lundman, 1974a, 1974b, 1979. Sherman, 1980, provides a comprehensive overview of the "causes" of police behavior.) In other words, these studies uniformly stop just short of the question of importance: What consequence does the behavior of the police officer have on the resolution of the incident, the solution of the crime, the rights of the suspect and victim, or the ability of the rest of the criminal justice system to process arrestees?

This is not to say that officer effectiveness has been totally ignored by previous research. A few attempts have been made to measure the quality of an officer's job performance. Each of these has taken a slightly different approach to developing operational indicators of officer performance.

Forst et al. (1977) are perhaps the most open about the problems of measuring how much an officer does or what effect these actions might have. They enunciate some of the limitations of such research:

> The police perform many different functions, not only in the area of crime control, but in several other areas of public service as well. To produce a single measure of productivity that encompasses all these functions is beyond hope.

> Even within the area of crime control, the measurement of an officer's performance is an awesome task. We really do not know how each of a particular officer's accomplishments contributes to the control of crime. Moreover, many of an officer's immediate accomplishments in this area are themselves not measurable. For example, suppose that an officer deals with a truant juvenile in a particularly creative and responsible way, so as to stimulate the eventual transformation of a borderline delinquent into a contributing member of society. The immediate police action in this instance—as well as the value that derives from it—will surely elude precise measurement [Forst et al., 1977: 47].

Many police activities will undoubtedly elude precise measurement. This does not mean that it is impossible to measure many things the police do or that we should give up now on a "hopeless" cause. Nor do Forst and his colleagues advocate such defeatism. They continue: " . . . it is clear that important aspects of police performance in the area of crime control *are* measurable" (Forst et al., 1977: 47). As an example of operational measures of effective police work, they advocate using two indicators. First, the quality of police arrests can be measured by the rate with which arrestees are convicted by the courts. They argue that if the officer does all the things necessary to assist the prosecutor to obtain a conviction, that is, if the officer recovers evidence and secures witnesses and does not make any unnecessary arrests, he will have maximized the chance of conviction of an offender, a primary duty in an attempt to control crime.[1] A second measure of officer effectiveness is the number of convictions attributable to the officer. This is a quantity dimension of effectiveness that should be directly related to a reduction in crime rates.

These measures of effectiveness only take into account one aspect of police service. Many other measures of effectiveness have been proposed. The following list presents just a few[2]:

Cohen and Chaiken (1972)

Career type
Awards
Harassment
Departmental charges
Citizen complaints
Criminal complaints
Total complaints
Trials
Substantiated complaints
Times sick
Injury disapproval
Firearms removal

Bloch and Anderson (1974)

Supervisory ratings
Activity levels
Injuries
Sick leave
Public comments
Observed officer demeanor
Observed citizen demeanor
Attitudes toward police work

Farr and Landy (1979)

Supervisory ratings
Peer Ratings
Job knowledge
Judgment
Use of equipment
Initiative
Dependability
Demeanor
Attitude
Relations with others
Communication

Froemel (1979)

Activity levels
Letters of commendation
Reprimands
Sick days
Departmental service ratings
Tenure
Education
Academy grade
Marksmanship
Citizen complaints
Chargeable accidents
Supervisory ratings

Spielberger et al. (1979)

Academy grades and class rank
Peer ratings
Supervisory ratings
Commendations
Reprimands
Promotions

Problems with this list should be readily apparent. There are an incredible number of possible indicators of police performance or police effectiveness. Which criteria should be emphasized? An answer to this question must contain two judgments. First, we obviously want to use those measures that are most reliable and valid; that is, we want to increase the odds that any judgment we make about a police officer based on the chosen indicators will be correct. Second, however, the response must be "It depends [on what you want the police to do]." If the police should be law enforcers, then perhaps Forst et al.'s conviction rate criterion is a legitimate measure of officer performance. Police supervisors, on the other hand, may exhibit a rationale typical of many bureaucrats. They may prefer not to rock the boat. Ability to follow orders, write coherent (and presumably accurate) reports, and generate numbers of activities (tickets, arrests, and so on) may be accurate indicators of officer effectiveness in their minds. The public may value other aspects of police work, with each neighborhood and interest group wishing for a different service emphasis (Whitaker, et al., 1982). In other words, the choice of effectiveness operationalization is based on perspective. Politics in the very general sense underlies choice of indicators.

Because of "politics" and because police do many different things, some have suggested using "multiple indicators" for evaluating police services. Undue concentration on single effectiveness indicators may result, according to this argument, in inaccurate conclusions about the quality of police service. This argument is only half true. One reason for using multiple indicators is that the measurement properties of the indicators can often be ascertained. With a single indicator of any construct we remain "blissfully unaware" of the extent and types of errors in our indicators (Blalock, 1970: 111).

The second argument used to justify multiple indicators is that failure to identify multiple measures of effectiveness leads to overemphasis on one police activity and underemphasis on all others. Skolnick (1966), for example, argues that police focus on clearance rates to the exclusion of other important aspects of police work. Whether multiple indicators are relevant to this situation depends on why clearance rates are important and why they were chosen as *the* criterion of importance in the first place. If someone or some group decides that police should only handle crime fighting situations and that they have carte blanche in doing whatever they see fit to reduce crime, then perhaps we only need a single indicator (or a set of indicators about a single police task) rather than multiple irrelevant measurements.

However, if we decide police do have multiple tasks and that it is important to measure each of them, the use of multiple indicators will likely render any choice process problematic. With a great deal of luck, it might be possible to use these indicators in such a way as to maintain effective behaviors and suppress ineffective ones. This situation would occur if the several performance indicators all agreed that one behavior was an effective method for dealing with a problem while another behavior was not. But real life usually contains some bad luck as well as good. A more likely situation is that some effectiveness measures will judge one behavior to be a valued one, while others suggest it is detrimental. A choice of which indicator is more important than the others then becomes the major problem for service improvement. Unfortunately, the political nature of this decision is often unrecognized by those attempting to upgrade police services.

Multiple indicators are not the final solution to police effectiveness assessment. Multiple indicators of the quality of a single aspect of police work evaluated from a single perspective may be useful in evaluating the quality of measurement. Indicators of multiple aspects of police work or indicators of a single police task evaluated from more than one vantage point may complicate the matter of assessment substantially. They do, however, identify the areas of disagreement in assessing police performance as well as indicate what types of changes would be preferred. Multiple indicators, therefore, may remove our ignorance about the measurement properties of our data, but they will also eliminate the blissfulness that accompanied that ignorance.

MEANS AND ENDS IN POLICING

Discrepancies between service goals and actual service levels often serve as a basis for criticisms of police services. But simply identifying a discrepancy does not tell us why the discrepancy exists. We must be able to identify the *process* by which police services are delivered in order to have some idea of where the process is deficient and to modify the process to do a better job in producing the service. In simple terms, we are concerned with the means by which police services are produced.

Recently, Herman Goldstein (1979) has questioned this means-ends approach to policing. He is not critical of the distinction between the two criteria, but rather is concerned with the overemphasis on the means of policing. Goldstein insists that police agencies suffer from a "means over ends" syndrome.

In discussing the history of attempts to improve policing in this country, Goldstein notes an almost exclusive concern with management reforms. Such an emphasis, he implies, is misplaced. The purpose and primary goal of policing is to serve citizens, and it is not clear that administrative streamlining furthers progress toward this goal.

> What is troubling is that administrators of those agencies that have succeeded in developing a high level of operating efficiency have not gone on to concern themselves with the end results of their efforts— with the actual impact that their streamlined organizations have on the problems the police are called upon to face.

> The police seem to have reached a plateau at which the highest objective to which they aspire is administrative competence [Goldstein, 1977: 239].

Police administrators need to recognize their *raison d'être* if policing is to be improved. However, the problem is not so much one of failure to understand the goals of policing as it is in a mistaken understanding of the process of achieving those goals. The failure of policing, we would suggest, is not an overemphasis of means over ends, but rather an emphasis on the "wrong" means for improving police service. Administrators have been too quick to grasp for means to improve the organization when it is not the organization that provides most police services, but rather the solitary officer on the street who does most of the work, who receives the least credit, and who must serve as the focal point of any attempt to change police services. Police service delivery has been analyzed all too frequently as a macro-level problem.

A much more productive approach to evaluating police services is to focus on the micro level. Goldstein's plea to remember the ends of our production process should not be forgotten.[3] But we would also concentrate on what immediately precedes the end state. The focus of our research, consequently, is the patrol officer-citizen encounter. The questions we ask are "What do police do in response to specific requests for service by citizens?" and "Is what the police do in response to these demands appropriate, satisfactory, effective?'

In attempting to answer both of these questions, many of the performance indicators and research designs used previously must be ruled out.

Most of those indicators are based on estimates of aggregate officer performance. It seems unlikely that some officers uniformly outperform their fellow officers in handling *all* types of problems. Different problems require different abilities that are unevenly distributed among patrol officers. In an effort to identify these differences, we evaluate officer performance in handling individual situations involving four problems typically faced by all officers.

Investigation of officer effectiveness in response to different types of problems is possible with certain types of effectiveness indicators that have been used previously by making them problem or situation specific. Thus, for example, Froemel (1979) offers a series of Job Performance Description Scales, some of which deal with an officer's response to domestic, traffic control, first aid, and crime prevention and detection situations. But these types of data fail to satisfy our needs for *process* information. Specifically, to be able to determine why an officer is effective or not, observational data are needed to find out how each officer deals with each problem he or she faces. Lacking such data, it is possible to relate officer characteristics to effectiveness ratings. In that situation, however, it is impossible to do more than attempt to screen certain types of individuals from the ranks of police officers. With data on the process of policing, we can (1) examine our notions as to what constitutes effective behavior, (2) modify that behavior where appropriate, and (3) train new recruits in preferred methods for handling specific problems. Thus, our examination of officer effectiveness is predicated on an ability to observe the officer's interaction with citizens in resolving the problems that initiate an encounter. Furthermore, interpretation of effectiveness assessments must focus on the means of policing if improvements are to be made.

Our study, consequently, involves the analysis of police activities in a variety of situations. Some of these involve crimes and others do not.[4] We concentrate on officer response to four general problems: Part I property crimes, disturbances, domestic problems, and interpersonal conflict other than domestic.[5] In addition, we focus only on encounters involving a single citizen and a police officer. The multicitizen situation is much more complex.[6]

The data analyzed here were collected as part of the Police Services Study, a joint project undertaken by researchers at Indiana University and the University of North Carolina.[7] Trained observers rode with patrol officers on 900 tours of duty (approximately 7400 hours). These officers were members of 24 departments that serve the St. Louis, Rochester, and Tampa-St. Petersburg metropolitan areas. During the observation period, we viewed 5688 encounters between police officers and citizens. For each of these encounters, observers filled out a Patrol Encounter Form (described in detail by Caldwell, 1978). Information coded on these forms serve as the principal data for our analyses. Of these 5688 encounters, 13.2 percent (1675) fall under one of our four general problems. Seven percent are property crime problems, while 4 percent are disturbances. Two percent of all encounters involve interpersonal conflict problems. Half of these are domestics, while half involve strangers.[8]

PATROL OFFICER EFFECTIVENESS

Rather than applying our own criteria to each officer's ability to deal with the problems he or she faces on the street, we permit those served by the officer to signal their judgments of the services police provide. During the observation of each police-citizen exchange, our fieldworkers coded several items designed to indicate citizen reaction to the officer. This information has been used to create three indicators of officer effectiveness: ability to reduce tension in the encounter, command of citizen respect, and expression of citizen satisfaction.

Operationalizations of Effectiveness

Effectiveness I: Emotional State

Citizens exhibit a variety of emotions during their encounters with police. The police officer, through actions and attitudes, may change a citizen's state of mind. We propose that one indicator of officer effectiveness is the officer's ability to reduce emotional tension. That is, we will judge an officer effective if he or she is able to induce emotional change during the course of the encounter so that the citizen is calm at its conclusion. On the other hand, we would consider an officer's behavior to be ineffective if the citizen began the encounter in an approximately calm state and became angry, violent, or upset (as a consequence of the officer's actions).

While expressed citizen emotions are used to define this indicator of effectiveness, the perspective underlying this indicator is that of the patrol supervisor. One of the many job skills valued by sergeants is an ability to keep incidents from escalating, and to decrease any violence potential among participants. Inability to alleviate tensions may lead to citizen complaints or to forcible arrests that may result in complaints or legal proceedings.

We can apply weaker evaluations of officer actions if citizen emotions do not change during the encounter. The effectiveness indicator suggested above implies that we wish officers to reduce tension by the end of the encounter; that is, we value a calm citizenry. But if the citizen appeared calm at the beginning and end of the encounter, we cannot attribute this positive state of mind to the officer's actions. The only inference that we might draw is that the police officer has not been ineffective, that is, has not done any emotional damage if a calm citizen remains so during the encounter. Alternatively, the officer has not been effective if the citizen began *and ended* the encounter angry or upset.

Thus, all citizens who exhibit relative calmness at the conclusion of an encounter have been served by either "effective" or "not ineffective" officers. The difference between these two evaluations depends on whether any change in emotional state was noticed by our trained observers. Angry or upset individuals, on the other hand, have been served by ineffective or not effective officers. Again, the different judgments of the officers depend on observed changes of the citizens' emotions. Our judgments of patrol officers can be summarized as follows:

Emotional States (Beginning-End)	Evaluation I
Angry-Calm	effective
Calm-Calm	not ineffective
Angry-Angry	not effective
Calm-Angry	ineffective

Effectiveness II: Demeanor Toward the Officer

Officer effectiveness may also be gauged in terms of the attitudes toward the officer that citizens express during the course of the encounter. Patrol officers are usually accorded considerable respect by most citizens. But a wide variety of demeanors are observed during police-citizen interactions.

Changes in citizen demeanor will be used to discriminate between effective and ineffective officers in the same way that change in emotional state is used to identify good and bad patrol officer. As in the case of citizens' emotions, officers (usually) are not directly responsible for the initial attitudes expressed upon their arrival. An officer's behavior and attitudes may, however, be crucial for the final demeanor displayed by the citizen.

The perspective underlying this indicator of officer effectiveness is that of the patrol officer. Numerous studies of officer-citizen interactions indicate that perhaps the most important demand an officer makes of a citizen is that the citizen exhibit some deference to the officer's authority (see especially Sykes and Clark, 1975). While most citizens also expect some reciprocity in offering respect, a process that has been labeled "deference exchange," it is true that officers hold most of the cards in an asymmetrical status relationship. This is especially true in poorer neighborhoods (Bittner, 1967).

Often officers experience stereotypic reactions to their appearance at the scene, reactions based on either the citizen's past experience with the police or the experiences with the police of the social group to whom he or she belongs. Officers, however, does have the potential to change the way citizens interact with them during the encounter. Their capacity to do so will be examined in this study. If hostile, detached, or sarcastic citizens can be induced to treat the officer with some respect by the end of the encounter, the patrol officer will be judged effective. (Of course, there are many ways for an officer to gain "respect." Thus, we will consider means as well as results.) If, on the other hand, citizens react to the officer's intrusion by becoming disrespectful or unconcerned, the officer will be rated ineffective.

As in the case of effectiveness based on citizen emotions, no change in attitudes expressed toward the police will provide a second measure differentiating officers. Judgments will be based on the demeanor maintained by the citizen over the course of the encounter. Friendly or businesslike individuals who remain so have been served by officers who will be judged "not ineffective." Sarcastic or hostile persons who do not change have met patrol officers who are "not effective."

Effectiveness III: Perceived Satisfaction

A third measure of officer effectiveness is provided by our observer's judgment of the citizen's evaluation of the service(s) provided by the officer: "Does the citizen give any evidence of satisfaction or dissatisfaction with the officer's actions?" Expressions of satisfaction redound to the officer's credit. Citizens' expressions of unhappiness with the services provided are considered to be indicative of poor performance by the officer. Quite obviously, this measure takes the citizen's perspective of the encounter although no explicit contact was made with the citizen to ascertain his or her opinion.

Each of the three operationalizations proposed above is based on the perceptions of neutral third-party observers. Parks (1981) has compared the perceptions of our observers and a sample of the citizens who took part in the encounters who were interviewed a week later. He found few differences in the reconstructions of events from the two perspectives.

Empirical Relationships Among Effectiveness Indicators

A cursory examination of the intercorrelations among our three indicators suggests that they do not measure the same thing. There is little consistency in the correlations in magnitude or direction. The interitem correlations between the effectiveness variables range from $-.04$ to $.70$ across the four types of problems. The mean interitem correlation among the effectiveness indicators is $.30$, although the mean varies considerably across problem type. The mean correlation for property crime encounters is $.08$, while it is $.52$ for domestic conflicts. This disagreement among our indicators should not be construed as a criticism of our effectiveness measures, however. One would not expect, for example, that easing tension *must* be correlated with citizen satisfaction. Consider the violent individual who becomes sedate after being arrested. In terms of our first criterion, the officer is judged to have reduced tension effectively in this situation. On the other hand, the arrested citizen is not likely to show appreciation for this decision.

OFFICER ACTIVITY:
A FIRST LOOK

A large portion of the patrol encounter form served as a checklist of specific actions taken by police officers. Some 11 actions not directed toward any individual citizen were tallied. These included such actions as conducting a search (with or without a warrant), calling for assistance (from other officers, medical and fire personnel, or auto maintenance crews) and report writing. For simplicity of presentation, these 11 activities are combined into 5 actions:

Searched premises

    Searched with a warrant
    Searched without a warrant
    Cursory look around scene

Service activity

    Call for ambulance
    Call for fire department
    Call for tow truck
    Removal of physical obstacles
    Direct traffic

Investigation

Protected scene
Questioned individuals away from scene

Took notes

Wrote Official report

Police actions are also directed at each citizen in the encounter. Forty-one separate activities were coded by our patrol observers. These ranged from arresting an individual, to physically or verbally threatening the citizen, to offering comfort and assistance, or referring the problem to someone who might help. Again, for simplicity, the 41 activities are presented as 23 patrol actions:

Arrest w/o force

Arrest at scene with warrant
Arrest at scene w/o warrant
Arrest at station

Arrest w/regular force

Arrest w/extraordinary force

Ticketed

Traffic ticket
Other ticket or citation

Detained at the scene

Searched citizen

Thorough search of citizen
Frisk of person

Asked citizen to sign a complaint

Questioned about the problem

Asked for about problem
Asked for name/description of suspect

Questioned about identification

Asked for reason at scene
Asked for identification

Force w/o arrest

Took by the arm
Made citizen come along
Handcuffed

Extraordinary Force w/o arrest

Hit with a weapon
Used force against citizen

Threatened

Threatened to hit
Threatened with gun
Threatened arrest
Threatened surveillance
Other threats
Shouted

Lectured

Talked into leaving the scene

Traffic alternatives

Written traffic warning
Verbal traffic warning

Comforted

Referred

Gave information on alternatives

    Gave crime prevention information

    Promised to provide additional information

Settled argument

Medical aid

    Took to doctor or hospital

    Gave first aid

Transported to another location (not station)

Provided information

Additional assistance

    Offered special police attention

    Gave some physical assistance

Officers will usually ask about a problem if they know what's going on. However, beyond this rather trivial action, no other action occurs with any substantial frequency. Police obviously play a significant role as information providers (25 percent of police-citizen contacts involve general or police related information, 17 percent involve alternative solutions, and 5 percent are direct referrals). The use of explicit legal authority occurs in relatively few situations (less than 2 percent of all citizens are arrested), although police powers are evident slightly more frequently (force is used in 2 percent of interactions, explicit threats in 5 percent, and lecturing in 12 percent).

The problem that necessitates police-citizen interaction has some impact on the choices made by patrol officers. A number of percentages vary considerably across the four problem types, indicating the relative popularity of an action for handling a given problem. These interproblem differences do not distract from the variation within problems of multiple choices of directed actions. Interproblem variation simply strengthens the argument that officers are capable of choosing from among alternatives to respond to the situations they face.

Taken together, these data permit two broad generalizations. First, a vast number of different activities are undertaken by patrol officers in the three metropolitan areas we studied. Furthermore, activity seemed to be discretionary; that is, no particular response is required of officers in all instances (at least with respect to the problems studied). Police do engage in a significant amount of questioning activity and do generate considerable paper in terms of report writing or note taking. Second, great variation in officer response exists across problems for many types of activity. Police officers do not react to all situations as automatons blindly following the same procedure no matter what problem arises. Not surprisingly, it appears that some attempt is made to respond to the exigencies of the particular situation.

But the reaction one must have to these data is "So what?" Whether we examine police behavior in terms of activity levels or the more perjorative term "discretionary actions," we have said very little of importance. The crucial question is: Does what patrol officers do on the street have any impact? Given that we know officers respond differently to diverse problems, we want to know if they make the right choices. The remainder of this chapter presents our preliminary attempt to evaluate officers' actions in handling problems arising from interpersonal conflicts, disturbances, property crimes, and domestic crises.

POLICE ACTIONS AND EFFECTIVENESS: A MULTIVARIATE APPROACH

In this section we examine the impact of each action on effectiveness. Rather than discuss the relationships between each police officer action and each effectiveness variable here, a discussion of the most and least effective police behaviors will be considered in a multiple regression framework. (The zero-order correlations between each effectiveness measure and each officer action are available from the authors. These relationships support the contention that the effectiveness indicators measure different components of police performance.) Table 1.1 presents a summary of the "sizable" unstandardized regression coefficients that relate patrol officer actions to citizen satisfaction in single-citizen encounters. All actions are coded as (1) officer performed this act or (0) officer did not perform this act. Citizen satisfaction is coded such that a high value is associated with greater satisfaction. Thus, a positive coefficient between an action and satisfaction would suggest that the action increased satisfaction and should therefore be judged effective. A negative coefficient, on the other hand, implies that action is associated with decreased satisfaction. Any action that reduces citizen satisfaction is considered ineffective here. We do not intend to repeat the contents of this table in the text. Rather, we will point out some of the noticeable trends and leave the reader to peruse the table at greater length.

What actions are ineffective in single citizen encounters? Very generally, and as one might expect, sanctioning behavior by law enforcement officials was likely to elicit lowered satisfaction (columns 3, 6, 9, and 12). Arrests, threats, the use of force, and ticketing all reduced citizen judgments of their police services. However, several assistance actions also have large negative coefficients and may, at first glance, appear puzzling. One

TABLE 1.1 The Multivariate Relationships of Officer Actions to Effectiveness

Officer Actions	Interpersonal Conflict			Property Crime			Disturbances			Domestic Conflict		
	ES	D	S	ES	D	S	ES	D	S	ES	D	S
Legal Sanctions												
Arrest w/o force	*	.34	-1.36				1.35	.24		-2.68	.63	-1.44
Arrest w/regular force	*	*	*			-.48	.26	-.69	-.47	-1.97	-.97	-1.21
Arrest w/extra force	*	*	*	.78	.56	-2.51	.51	.17	-.94	*	*	*
Ticketed	*	*				-.25		-.93	-.82	*	*	*
Detained at scene	-1.38		-.85	-.21	-.39		-.47	-.36	-.43	1.88	-.31	-1.30
Searched citizen	*	*	*	.19	.43	.51		-.23	-.44		-.10	.30
Asked to sign complaint										.30		.45
Questioned about problem			.38									.10
Questioned identification	.30		.14			.12	-.29			.26		-.33
Extralegal Sanctions												
Force w/o arrest	*	*	*	-.60	-.74	-.77	-.20	.11	-.16	.85	.85	-.52
Extraordinary force	*	*	*	*	*	*	*	*	*	*	*	*
Threatened	.38		-.15			-.22	-.10	-.12	-.28	1.17		
Lectured	-.34		.10			-.32			-.19	-.34	-.26	-.11
Talked into leaving	.89		-.17	.59					-.17	.13		
Traffic alternatives	*	*	*	*	*	*	.38	.49	.60	*	*	*

Assistance

	ES	D	ES	D	ES	D	ES	D	S	ES	D	S
Comforted	.11				.30		.35			.11	.11	.50
Referred	-.48	-.49			-.12	-.45	-.37			-.41	-.40	-.11
Gave info. on alternatives							.17			-.10	-.69	.38
Settled argument	.86		.20		*	*	.72	.55		*	*	-.15
Medical aid	.60	.48	-.23		*	*	-1.13			*	*	*
Transported			.17		-.40	-.64				-.49	-.35	-.67
Provided information					.28	.16		-.43		.17		-.23
Additional assistance	.16				.15	.13	.25	.16		.33		.46

Undirected Actions

	ES	D	ES	D	ES	D	ES	D	S	ES	D	S
Searched premises	-.31		-.16		.10		-.27			.13	.11	.63
Investigation	.40		.15		-.19		.10			.75		-.21
Took notes			.28				-.15					
Wrote official report		-.44	.12									.28
Additional services	.21	.40	.12		.85	-.60	.42	-.84		.46	.49	.28
R²	.35	.40	.34	.16	.21	.46	.36	.47		.60	.63	.64
N	81		81		375		234			61		

NOTE: ES = Emotional State: D = Citizen Demeanor; S = Citizen Satisfaction;
* indicates that no officer actions of this type were observed in these encounters.

37

wonders, for example, why medical assistance should have such a negative effect on satisfaction in disturbance situations. What is likely happening in these encounters is that the transportation of inebriates to formal or informal detoxification facilities is considered (at the time of the incident) to be functionally equivalent to the detention or arrest of the citizen. That is, the drunk feels his or her civil rights have been violated. Similarly, asking a citizen to sign a complaint may be a request with which the citizen does not wish to comply. Often, especially in interpersonal conflict or disturbance situations, citizens will request the informal use of police authority to quiet a street corner or restrain combatants, but do not wish to invoke any formal process.

. If sanctioning behavior is ineffective (from the citizen's perspective), what actions are judged positively? Basically, effective police responses to the four problems we examined include expressions of concern (such as promises of special attention, provision of information on crime or alternative services produced, and comfort and solace), attention to the problem (that is, the officer questioned the citizen about the problem, searched the premises, conducted additional investigation away from the scene of the encounter, and took an official report of the problem), and service activities and informal sanctions (lectures or warnings).

These are, of course, generalizations about the positive and negative effects of officer actions. Note, for example, that asking the citizen to sign a complaint is judged an effective act in domestic situations and an ineffective act in disturbances. A battered wife may want the *opportunity* to sign a complaint against her husband even if she decides not to do so or withdraws her signature later. Most disturbances, on the other hand, are not considered serious enough to warrant such sanctioning. As a second example, referral is positively rated as a response to disturbances, while it is considered an ineffective response to a domestic crisis. Referral to a detoxification center may provide the alcoholic with an immediate response to his or her drinking problem. Referral to a social service agency to deal with marital problems will probably not satisfy an individual concerned with the immediate confrontation.[9]

One ineffective officer activity deserves special attention. The use of extraordinary force by patrol officers is a combination of two observed actions. The first is the officer hitting the citizen with a weapon—a gun, nightstick, or heavy flashlight sometimes carried in place of a nightstick. The second is the use against the citizen of force not typically associated with arrest, that is, not involving handcuffing the citizen or the traditional taking by the arm to make the citizen move in the required direction. Three comments are in order. We do not, without examination of the narratives of the encounters, classify such behavior as "police brutality," although such implications might be drawn from the data with further study. Extraordinary force was not used without arrest in these encounters. We do not know, however, whether arrest is used to "cover" the officer for such behavior. Second, such behavior is extremely rare (and we do not believe that to be a function of officer reactivity to patrol observation). Third, while extremely infrequent, this type of force has a very significant negative impact on citizen judgments. Arrest-oriented force, in contrast, was evaluated much less harshly.

Having discussed our findings regarding the relationship between citizen satisfaction and officer actions in some detail, we will merely summarize the results of the regressions of officer actions on citizen emotional state and demeanor quite briefly, noting principally the different types of activities that receive high ratings across the different evaluative criteria.

Table 1.1 identifies those police actions most strongly related to changes in citizen emotional state in single-citizen encounters (columns 1, 4, 7, and 10). This criterion may be used to evaluate police activities from the perspective of the patrol supervisor. The ability to communicate with and express understanding of the problems of citizens is certainly one skill valued by a patrol officer's superiors (Farr and Landy, 1979). Such skill implies an ability to defuse emotional situations. The actions displayed in Table 1.1 suggest that certain activities appear very useful in this regard. However, the impact of an action is often dependent on the type of problem it is used to resolve. Medical assistance helps calm citizens in single-citizen conflict situations, but it increases tensions dramatically when used during disturbances. Arrest is a positively valued means of dealing with property crimes and disturbances, but not conflict situations.

In Table 1.1, the relationships between officer activities and changes of citizen demeanor in single-citizen encounters are also presented (columns 2, 5, 8, and 11). Here we return to the perspecitve of the patrol officer in evaluating police services. What can the officer do to maximize respect, offered grudgingly or otherwise, for his or her authority? As should be expected given our previous results, the answer to this question depends on what type of problem the officer is trying to resolve. A number of activities raise respect levels in some situations and lower them in others. Arrest and the use of force, for example, improve citizen demeanor toward the officer in conflict and property crime encounters. However, the same actions only exacerbate any misgivings an individual may have toward the officer and the authority he or she represents in disturbance and domestic situations.

Having examined Table 1.1 for specific actions relevant to specific problems, we also wish to examine the degree to which police actions explain effectiveness ratings. At the bottom of each column in Table 1.1 is the percentage of the variance of the effectiveness measure explained by the regression of effectiveness on all officer actions. Effectiveness ratings in single-citizen encounters are generally well explained by police officer actions. With the exception of the relationships between emotional state and police actions in property crime encounters, and between citizen satisfaction and actions also for property crime encounters, approximately 35 to 65 percent of the variation in effectiveness may be accounted for by officer actions. Nevertheless, there is some substantial variation in the impact of police actions in response to different problems. Police actions appear to have greater effect in interpersonal and domestic conflict problems. However, there are relatively few single-citizen encounters that involve these problems. Thus, the high coefficients of determination reflect, in part, the limited degrees of freedom available in these data.

CONCLUSION

In this chapter we have attempted to make two principal statements. First, whether we want them or not, many indicators of officer effectiveness or performance exist. To that already impressive list of indicators, we are willing to add additional measures for assessing patrol officers. Second, the major contribution of this chapter is its attempt to relate officer activity to evaluations of effectiveness. Theoretically, an ability to make such judgments should permit modifications in police service delivery in such a way as to maximize the probability that changes have desired impacts. Empirically, assessing police officers this way remains difficult. Difficulty, however, should not preclude attempts to understand the process by which patrol officers provide police services.

We have also mentioned a problem that is inadequately considered by many of those engaged in evaluating all types of social programs and services. Multiple indicators of effectiveness, let alone any other general evaluative criterion, will probably yield different assessments of any particular officer action. How we pick and choose among preferred activities is a political problem and must be dealt with as such. All too often implementors assume that this political process is irrelevant to decisions to improve service delivery. But one person's improvement in service is another's reduction. Appeals to professionalism are not adequate substitutes for the resolution of diverse interests in the delivery of police services. We do not try to do so here. Our task at this point is to try to understand how the process of service delivery can be improved from diverse and perhaps divergent perspectives. Decisions over priorities, however, will perhaps be more critical, and more difficult, in the long run.

NOTES

1. Conviction rates, of course, have been criticized, as have most operational indicators of police performance. One major problem with convictions or conviction rates as a measure of performance is that police have only partial control over the outcome of any case. Convictions are dependent on the resources of the prosecutor's office as well as the willingness of other parties to cooperate. Judges may manage their dockets by agreeing to plea bargaining arrangements. Thus, conviction rates may best be seen as an indicator of the effectiveness of the criminal justice system rather than just police officers. Criticisms might still be raised, however, as convictions also depend on citizen input; for example, witnesses and victims must become involved.

2. For additional officer performance measures, see Allen and Maxfield, Chapter 3 in this volume.

3. Specifically, Goldstein asserts that police tend to measure their performance in terms of the frequency with which they employ easily quantifiable means of solving a problem, rather than in terms of the degree to which the problem is solved. Police in a jurisdiction characterized by chronic double parking, for example, tend to evaluate their performance by counting the number of parking tickets issued, rather than by assessing the degree to which their efforts have reduced actual double-parking violations. Emphasis on tickets as "means" to the "end" of reducing double parking is important, he would argue, but diverts attention from the degree to which the problem is solved and from other less easily quantifiable and possibly more effective means—warnings, public education, and the like—to the same end.

4. There is, of course, some question about observational definitions of crime: Who defines it? If one allows the police to define the law, Black argues that one must conclude that enforcement is total. Acceptance of such a definition of crime precludes the study of discretion. Observer or citizen definitions of crime, on the other hand, suggest professional judgments by nonprofessionals. In our research, we prefer to study problems presented to the police rather than crimes.

5. Each of the police-citizen encounters that we observed was coded using one or more of 236 problem identifiers. Each of the four general problem types studied in this chapter might have been coded in a number of ways. The specific problem codes that fall within each of the four general problem types are:

Interpersonal Conflict	nondomestic argument
	physical injury (and threat)
	nondomestic assault
	nondomestic fight
	nondomestic aggravated assault

Major Property Crimes	theft and attempted theft
	purse snatch/pickpocket
	burglary
	break-in and attempted break-in
Disturbances	public nuisance
	drunk
	disorderly
	vagrancy
	loitering
	obscene activity
	noise
	begging/peddling
	harassment
Domestic Conflict	domestic argument
	domestic fight
	domestic assault
	domestic aggravated assault

The rationale behind the coding of encounters and a detailed explanation of the type of problem that falls within each specific incident code are described in an appendix available from the authors.

6. A preliminary examination of the multiple-citizen encounter is presented in a paper by the authors (McIver and Parks, 1982). Unfortunately, lack of space precluded any discussion of police effectiveness in such encounters here.

7. Phase II of the Police Services Study, in which these data were collected, was conducted with funding from the National Science Foundation under grant number NSF GI 43949 and from the National Institute of Justice under grant number 78-NI-AX-0020. This support is gratefully acknowledged.

8. There are substantially more interpersonal conflict situations experienced by the police. Such encounters involve more than one citizen, however, and are excluded from this analysis.

9. For an extended examination of police referral practices, see Scott, 1981.

REFERENCES

BITTNER, E. (1967) "The police on skid row: A study of peace keeping." American Sociological Review 32: 699-715.

BLACK, D. J. (1970) "The production of crime rates." American Sociological Review 35: 733-748.

––– (1980) The Manner and Customs of the Police. New York: Academic Press.

––– and A. J. REISS (1970) "Police control of juveniles." American Sociological Review 35: 63-77.

BLALOCK, H. M. (1970) "Estimating measurement error using multiple indicators and several points in time." American Sociological Review 35: 101-111.

BLOCH, P. B. and D. ANDERSON (1974) Policewomen on Patrol. Washington, DC: Police Foundation.

CALDWELL, E. (1978) "Patrol observation: the patrol encounter, patrol narrative, and general shift information forms." Police Services Study Methods Report MR-02. Bloomington, IN: Indiana University, Workshop in Political Theory and Policy Analysis.

COHEN, B. and J. M. CHAIKEN (1972) Police Background Characteristics and Performance. Lexington, MA: D. C. Heath.

FARR, J. L. and F. J. LANDY (1979) "The development and use of supervisory and peer scales for police performance appraisal," in C. D. Spielberger (ed.) Police Selection and Evaluation. New York: Praeger.

FORST, B., J. LUCIANOVIC, and S. J. COX (1977) What Happens After Arrest? Washington, DC: Institute for Law and Social Research.

FRIEDRICH, R. J. (1980) "Police use of force: individuals, situations, and organizations." The Annals of The American Academy of Political and Social Science 452: 82-97.

FROEMEL, E. C. (1979) "Objective and subjective measures of police officer performance," in C. D. Spielberger (ed.) Police Selection and Evaluation. New York: Praeger.

GOLDSTEIN, H. (1977) Policing a Free Society. Cambridge, MA: Ballinger.

――― (1979) "Improving policing: a problem-oriented approach." Crime and Delinquency 25: 236-258.

LUNDMAN, R. J. (1974a) "Domestic police-citizen encounters." Journal of Police Science and Administration 2: 22-27.

――― (1974b) "Routine police arrest practices: a commonweal perspective." Social Problems 22 (October): 127-141.

――― (1979) "Organizational norms and police discretion: an observational study of police work with traffic law violators." Criminology 17: 159-171.

MANNING, P. K. (1977) Police Work. Cambridge, MA: MIT Press.

McIVER, J. P. and R. B. PARKS (1982) "Effective and ineffective uses of patrol officer discretion," presented at the annual meetings of the Academy of Criminal Justice Sciences, Louisville, Kentucky, March 23-27.

PARKS, R. B. (1981) "Comparing citizen and observer perceptions of police-citizen encounters," presented at the annual meeting of the Southeastern American Society for Public Administration, Jackson, Mississippi, October 15-16.

REISS, A. J. (1971) The Police and the Public. New Haven, CT: Yale University Press.

SCOTT, E. J. (1981) Police Referral in Metropolitan Areas: Summary Report. Washington, DC: National Institute of Justice.

SHERMAN, L. W. (1980) "Causes of police behavior: the current state of quantiative research." Journal of Research in Crime and Delinquency 17: 69-100.

SKOLNICK, J. H. (1966) Justice Without Trial: Law Enforcement in a Democratic Society. New York: John Wiley.

SPIELBERGER, C. D., J. C. WARD, and H. C. SPAULDING (1979) "A model for the selection of law enforcement officers," in C. D. Spielberger (ed.) Police Selection and Evaluation. New York: Praeger.

SYKES, R. E. and J. P. CLARK (1975) "A theory of deferrence exchange in police-civilian encounters." American Journal of Sociology 81: 584-600.
WHITAKER, G. P. et al. (1982) Measuring Police Agency Performance. Washington, DC: U.S. Government Printing Office.
WILSON, J. Q. (1968) Varieties of Police Behavior: The Management of Law and Order in Eight Communities. New York: Atheneum.

2.

POLICE KNOWLEDGE OF THE PATROL BEAT:
A Performance Measure

Stephen Mastrofski

Pennsylvania State University

Traditional measures of police performance stress the apprehension of offenders and the deterrence of crime, but numerous recent studies show that police do much more than fight crime, and few demonstrate any police capacity to reduce it. Several recent works call for a reorientation in police performance assessment. They reject intangible and unvalidated performance indicators and express the need to develop measures that are more tangible and within police capacity to influence (Kelling, 1978; Whitaker et al., 1980; Wycoff, 1982). This chapter argues that police officer knowledge of the beat is a concept that could form one basis for this sort of performance measurement. First discussed are the reasons that police have excluded beat knowledge from formal performance evaluations. Second, a conceptual basis for measuring officer knowledge of the beat is proposed. Third, research on several current management strategies that might influence beat knowledge are reviewed. Finally, additional empirical evidence is presented on the impact of organizational arrangements on one indicator of beat knowledge: officers' awareness of citizen organizations dealing with crime and police problems on their beats.

Author's Note: *Partial support for this chapter was received from the National Institute of Justice, U.S. Department of Justice, under Grant 80-IJ-CX-0014. Points of view or opinions stated herein are the author's and do not necessarily represent the official position or policies of the U.S. Department of Justice. The author thanks Richard Bennett and Gordon P. Whitaker for their comments on a draft of this chapter.*

THE PROFESSIONAL CONSENSUS

Although knowledge of the beat is not part of the arsenal of performance indicators traditionally used to defend police agencies' budgets and programs, there is a long-standing consensus on its importance to police work. Police manuals dating from the nineteenth century to the present stress the need for the patrol officer to develop a personal knowledge of people, places, and customs. In the nineteenth century, the foot patrolman was expected to use his knowledge to maintain order. After the conversion to automotive patrol, "good government" reformers, such as O.W. Wilson, emphasized the need for the patrol officer to know the "hazards" on the beat and to develop information sources to fight crime and maintain order (Wilson, 1963: 237). Professional reformers of the 1960s and 1970s presented the acquisition of beat knowledge as a way of improving community relations as well as fighting crime (Murphy and Plate, 1977; Gay et al., 1977; Davis, 1978). Many reformers in the neighborhood movement hoped that a stronger and more personalized police effort to know the neighborhoods would facilitate a professional response "shaped more closely to the tastes of the residents" and perhaps ultimately produce a service delivery more sensitive to grass-roots control (Schmandt, 1972: 577). Even the occupational culture of the rank-and-file officer places detailed knowledge of the beat at the top of the list of requisite tools for patrol. Several ethnographies and "realistic" accounts of police work emphasize the centrality of beat knowledge for apprehending offenders, maintaining order, and ensuring the safety of the officer (Van Maanen, 1974; Rubinstein, 1973; Wambaugh, 1972). From a variety of perspectives, police knowledge of the beat is the sine qua non of effective street work.

Despite this broad consensus on the importance of beat knowledge, police departments have not institutionalized it in their formal evaluations of personnel or agency performance, because it does not accord with the occupation's dominant view of what constitutes professionalism. The police aspiration or claim to professional status is a claim to exclusive access to a specific body of knowledge and technical expertise "acquired from academic investigation, experimentation and research" (Menke et al., 1982: 79). There is no occupational consensus on the precise composition of this knowledge and expertise, but contemporary professional views are clearly grounded in the belief that policing should be based on generalizable principles of science. This can be interpreted as part of the attempt by reformers to change the occupation's status from craft (where particularistic knowledge is required to deal with highly idiosyncratic situations) to science (where the appropriate police action can be justified by general theories and predicted with regularity). The profession nurtures scientifically tested methods for handling medical emergencies, domestic crises, sex offenders, hostage situations, collecting evidence, and so forth. The evidence of the predominance of this scientific view of the profession's knowledge base can be found in police academies, training manuals, professional journals, and department SOPs.

The precepts of craftsmanship are much different from those of professionalism. The craftsman's view of policing is like that of a river pilot. Knowledge of scientific theory (such as hydraulics and propulsion) is secondary to intimate knowledge of the territory (the river). Knowing the subtle, ever-changing nuances of a neighborhood's people, places, and practices enhances the capacity of the police officer-as-craftsperson to make the right decisions about when and how to intervene, how to respond to people, when to be legalistic, and when to "use discretion." Adhering to this view of patrol work, one must accept the limitations of abstract, highly generalized science. This is troublesome for many professional reformers, for they have wed this perspective to a bureaucratic one (see Menke et al., 1982). The generalizability of scientific knowledge allows administrators greater flexibility in making work assignments: A knowledgeable officer can work any beat. It is more efficient and seems fairer in evaluating personnel: A knowledgeable officer can be promoted based on a standardized exam. Police professionalism views science as a means of restricting the discretion of street-level officers. To accept the idiosyncratic view of street work is to acknowledge the administrator's tenuous claim to control decision making based on a widely possessed body of knowledge. Isolated at headquarters, managers have scarcely more claim to the necessary knowledge of a particular beat than does the average citizen—and substantially less than the officers who work there. This subverts not only the legitimacy of police managers to perform a critical bureaucratic function; it also threatens the long-cherished professional value of autonomy from political influence.

The irony of the real locus of control in the street-level bureaucracy of policing (Prottas, 1978) is a bitter pill for most administrators to swallow. But recognizing the importance of the craftsman's need for particularistic knowledge would help infuse administrators with a more productive view of their management function than the widely embraced bureaucratic control perspective. Craftsmen are developed, not controlled. Encouraging officers to pursue intimate knowledge of their beats is a step toward developing a better capacity among police for exercising discretion. While this would not supplant the need for other measures to manage discretion, including attempts to develop and disseminate a police science, it would directly address the uncertainty and ambiguity that is necessarily part of the patrol officer's workday. There is a broad but unharnessed consensus that the patrol officer's intimate knowledge of the beat is instrumental to the achievement of many organizational goals: detection and apprehension of offenders, maintenance of order, appropriate use of force, and responsiveness to client needs. The American democratic tradition calls for a government of officials who know and understand their public. Routine police performance evaluation should reflect these values by using indicators of this knowledge.

A CONCEPTUALIZATION OF BEAT KNOWLEDGE

What is beat knowledge? Certainly it is familiarity with the people and places within given geographic boundaries, as Rubinstein (1973) and Van Maanen (1974) suggest, but it can be more than that: It can be a down-to-earth theory of human behavior. William K. Muir suggests that a police officer's knowledge of people and events has two components: judgment and understanding. Judgment refers to a straightforward, factual awareness that permits officers to predict events with accuracy. Judgment is knowing what goes on in the beat—who belongs where and when. It is knowing the patterns of neighborhood life. Understanding refers to a more abstract awareness or interpretation of the human condition applied to immediate circumstances. It refers to the ability to "see the play of the many motives involved. . . . Understanding constitute[s] the know-how, the knowledge of cause and effect, in short, the technology of governing" (Muir, 1977: 173).

An example may help distinguish these two components. A patrol officer sees a group of juveniles at a street corner in a busy part of the business district of his beat. *Judgment* tells the officer that they gather there frequently and that they seldom—but do occasionally—cause trouble. The officer *understands* that the juveniles gather there to shoot the breeze about school, girlfriends and boyfriends, sports, and so on. The location is ideal for them because it is near the school (but far enough to be beyond the control of school officials), near a convenience store, and is the central part of the "public" part of town, through which many of their peers pass on the way to school, work, or play. This is where their "society" passes. The group has a strong attachment to this area because of its advantageous location. The group would not find a less obtrusive spot, such as a nearby park, palatable. The only occasions when the group has gotten out of hand have been when a gang from an adjacent neighborhood intruded. The intruding group's membership is older and more belligerent than this one. Neighborhood retailers have become increasingly apprehensive about juvenile gangs, although their relationship with the neighborhood's group has not become too strained, because they are a significant source of income for some merchants. In sum, this group is controllable and a beneficial part of the neighborhood under usual conditions. The officer's understanding of the situation allows him or her to distinguish different types of juvenile groups, seeing both their threat and value to the community. This understanding of the juvenile situation is ultimately a theory about what makes these people tick. Armed with understanding and judgment, the officer is in a position to govern the beat effectively. He or she will have a sense of the need for intervention in this instance and will also sense the distribution of probable outcomes of the various alternatives: ignoring the juveniles, rapping with them, lecturing them, suggesting an alternative rendezvous, ordering them to disperse, and so forth.

The ultimate choice of strategies in the foregoing example is guided by the officer's values and the threats and rewards (from the department and businesspeople) he or she anticipates. Consequently, a knowledgeable officer may make an inappropriate choice if his or her values are inconsistent with those of the evaluator (sergeant, chief, fellow officer, neighborhood businesspeople, or the parents of the juveniles). Clearly, knowledge of this sort is no guarantee of performance. It is a necessary if not sufficient condition, however, and might therefore become part of the appraisal of the officer's and department's performance. Officers who are motivated to do so can use their knowledge to minimize the need for force, increase the utility of force that they do use, and increase the effectiveness of the assistance they render to citizens.

ORGANIZATIONAL INFLUENCES

A variety of organizational arrangements may have some impact on the knowledge patrol officers have of their beats. Seven such factors are considered here: department size, stability of beat assignments, residency requirements, personnel retention, officer beat assignment by race, community development, and special "beat development" programs.

The size of a police department seems to have an important bearing on the approach to patrol work its officers take (Brown, 1981; Parks, 1980;

Mastrofski, 1981b). Police in smaller jurisdictions tend to be more client-oriented and more familiar with neighborhood residents. The presumed intimacy of the small town may increase the ability and motivation of officers to acquire beat knowledge. To the extent that this is true, attempts to consolidate small police departments may make it difficult for street officers to acquire such knowledge.

Programs that decentralize patrol in large jurisdictions may diminish the alienating effects of large departments in large jurisdictions. Team policing and stable beat assignment plans are intended to facilitate officers' contacts and familiarity with neighborhood residents, leaders, and organizations (Gay et al., 1977). Research results are mixed. The Cincinnati team policing experiment evaluation indicates that stabilizing patrol assignments increased patrol officers' self-reported recognition of neighborhood residents but had very little impact on citizens' perceptions of officers' familiarity with neighborhood residents (Schwartz and Clarren, 1978: III-45). A study of patrol organization in 42 urban residential neighborhoods found that, regardless of neighborhood character, the more closely the organizational structure resembled a stable or neighborhood policing arrangement, the more likely officers were to show their acquaintance with citizens they encountered on the beat (Mastrofski, 1981a).

A variety of policies focused on the individual officer are often advocated to improve police performance. Some departments impose residency requirements, ostensibly to increase the officer's commitment to the community he or she polices. The hiring of "locals" is also a way that departments can increase the likelihood that the patrol force will be familiar with the beats.

The willingness and ability of departments to retain experienced officers may affect the pool of "knowledgeable" officers on the force. The effects of experience differ on police, so the impact of having a more experienced force is doubtlessly complex. In his fictionalized accounts of police life, Joseph Wambaugh (1972) tends to present the more experienced officers as having greater respect for beat knowledge, but extended experience can also produce a burnout that discourages continued pursuit of contact with the public or flexibility in adapting perceptions in changing beat conditions.

A frequent recommendation of study commissions on urban violence and criminal justice is to increase the representation of ethnic minority police officers, particularly in minority neighborhoods. Minority police ranks have grown substantially in some cities, but minorities are still generally underrepresented. Advocates of increased minority representation expect that these police officers can more easily understand problems in minority communities. Interviews with police and citizens suggest that black police officers are more interested in the black community and are more sympathetic to the black public than are white officers, but other research highlights the isolation of the black officer in the ghetto (Jacobs and Cohen, 1978). Placed between the two hostile forces of the department and the black community, the officer wants support from both (Cooper, 1980: Ch. 5). It is not clear whether these conditions encourage minority officers to develop knowledge of their beats. Their sense of isolation coupled with the expectation that they *should* have a greater knowledge may encourage them to establish communication channels in the neighborhood—perhaps through institutions traditionally acceptable to the department, such as churches, block groups, and crime prevention groups. However, their sense of isolation and the pressure to conform to the values of their more numerous white colleagues and supervisors may be great enough to prevent any appreciable difference.

Developing stronger and more diverse communication channels to the community has been a focus of police reform in the last fifteen years (Myren, 1972: 724). Department-sponsored community relations programs with the ostensible purpose of conducing police-citizen dialogue are usually geared more to changing the perceptions of citizens than to developing police perceptions and understanding citizens' problems (Goldstein, 1977: 8). Nevertheless, many neighborhood policing projects have attempted to establish systematic communication with neighborhood organizations where they are weak or nonexistent. Officers have been encouraged to consult neighborhood councils, church groups, and the like to monitor community concerns and preferences. These programs are intended to encourage citizen participation, increase the visibility of citizen groups, and ultimately provide the police with ready access to contacts who will enhance their judgment and understanding of the community (see Pomerleau, 1982: 205).

Few departments have instituted operational policies that reward officers for developing beat knowledge, and fewer still allocate adequate resources for effective implementation. Police administrators are reluctant to venture from the traditional reward structures embedded in arrests, citations, response time, and "keeping the lid on." Feeling the pressure from escalating demands for service, those who recognize the merit of developing beat knowledge are hard pressed to give officers the time to develop and share it. An exception is the San Diego Community Profile Project conducted in 1973-1974, which had as a principal goal "increasing the individual patrol officer's awareness and understanding of the community the officer serves" (Boydstun and Sherry, 1975: 1). Conducted as a controlled experiment, the project provided training and resources to encourage officers in the test group to obtain beat knowledge through close interaction with the community, access to department-supplied beat statistics, and sharing information with each other in group discussions. The acquisition of beat knowledge was a conspicuous part of the supervisors' personnel evaluation system. Officers in the control group were provided no special incentives or resources. After a year, the test group showed a significant gain compared to the control group in self-reported knowledge of physical, demographic, and socioeconomic characteristics of the beats and the availability and quality of community resources.

The empirical research on strategies for enhancing beat knowledge has stressed officers' familiarity with people, places, neighborhood characteristics, and available services. Clearly, these are not equivalent to the conceptualization of knowledge suggested by Muir. They constitute neither judgment of the likelihood of events nor appreciation of their etiology. Measures directly reflecting these sorts of knowledge require a thorough compilation of observations and neighborhood-by-neighborhood analysis to form a knowledge base against which individual officers serving specific beats can be assessed. Even the ambitious San Diego project relied on self-reported changes in knowledge rather than independent assessments. The resource requirements of such an evaluation are considerable and will be discussed in the concluding section of the chapter. Here it is sufficient to note that in the absence of direct indicators of judgment and understanding, it is useful to use proxy measures that are likely associated with judgment and understanding. The following empirical analysis relies on such a measure: police knowledge of citizen organizations on the beat.

AN EMPIRICAL ANALYSIS OF POLICE KNOWLEDGE OF CITIZEN ORGANIZATIONS

In a recent article in the *Atlantic Monthly,* James Q. Wilson and George L. Kelling wonder to what extent police street activity should be shaped by the neighborhood and the values that predominate in it. They appear to be calling for a greater emphasis on police responsiveness to neighborhood standards—as opposed to the abstract and distant "rules of the state" (1982: 34). To be responsive to neighborhood standards, police must have some knowledge of them, and this in turn requires some channel to communicate, clarify, and interpret diverse community values. One way is for officers to develop extensive personal contacts with residents and habitués and from their experiences develop their judgment and understanding of the community. Another is for officers to rely on citizen organizations in the neighborhood to aggregate, distill, and interpret the neighborhood's customs, events, and standards. These organizations promote citizen participation in both the formal and informal control of the neighborhood. Some emphasize the independent production of services to the neighborhood; others emphasize integration of their activities with government programs; others perform an advocacy function for members of the neighborhood vis-à-vis local government (see Sharp, 1978). These organizations in particular may color the officer's understanding of the threat of potential "hazards" (juvenile groups, winos, the mentally deranged, and other real and symbolic threats to public order). Contact with these groups should expand the informal resources available to an officer in solving situational crises, apprehending offenders, and maintaining acceptable levels of order. The officer's knowledge of these voluntary citizen organizations is thus a prerequisite for tapping into the social structure of the community he or she governs.

The Sample and Methods

The empirical analysis is based on data collection by the Police Services Study (PSS)[1] conducted in 1977 in 24 police departments located in Rochester, New York, St. Louis, Missouri, and Tampa-St. Petersburg, Florida. These departments were selected to represent a wide range in size and organizational structure in medium-sized metropolitan areas. They included 21 municipal and 3 county sheriff's departments.

Data collection focused on a sample of residential neighborhoods served by each department. Neighborhoods were selected to approximate the range of patrol service conditions in each jurisdiction, based on neighborhood wealth and racial makeup. Sixty neighborhoods (all predominantly residential) were selected, the larger jurisdictions being more heavily sampled than the smaller ones. Neighborhood boundaries were defined by beat boundaries in most instances.[2] Table 2.1 lists the participating departments.

Several data collection techniques were used. Samples of officers routinely assigned to each study neighborhood were interviewed—894 respondents in all. The in-person interview schedule covered questions about the officer's personal characteristics, professional history, work assignment, attitudes toward police work, and perceptions of the study neighborhood. A subsample of officers serving each neighborhood was observed by ride-along observers (approximately 120 hours per neighborhood). Observers recorded how and where officers spent their time and detailed informa-

TABLE 2.1   The Police Services Study Departments

Police Jurisdiction	Jurisdiction Population	No. of Study Neighborhoods	No. of Sworn Officers	No. Officers Interviewed
Kinloch, MO	5,600	1	15	12
Pinelawn, MO	5,700	1	13	9
Wellston, MO	5,800	1	24	14
Northwoods, MO	8,700	1	18	12
Brentwood, MO	10,000	2	23	9
Tarpon Springs, FL	11,400	2	23	13
Crestwood, MO	15,300	1	28	18
Berkeley, MO	18,300	2	38	19
Bridgeton, MO	24,000	1	51	10
Ferguson, MO	26,900	2	54	28
Pinellas Park, FL	29,400	1	33	17
Gates, NY	29,900	1	22	9
Kirkwood, MO	33,600	2	53	17
University City, MO	47,000	3	80	27
Largo, FL	54,900	2	53	30
Clearwater, FL	77,000	3	158	59
Greece, NY	84,100	1	68	16
Monroe Co., NY	185,300	2	203	45
Pinellas Co., FL	209,700	4	232	77
St. Petersburg, FL	236,400	4	453	80
Rochester, NY	259,000	7	646	73
Tampa, FL	296,700	5	595	124
Hillsborough Co., FL	330,200	3	283	50
St. Louis, MO	498,700	8	2,050	126

tion on their encounters with the public. A random sample of approximately 200 residents were interviewed by telephone in each study neighborhood. The survey included questions about household experiences with criminal victimization in the previous year, race and income characteristics of the household, and knowledge of citizen organizations active in the neighborhood. Police administrators were interviewed according to a loosely structured, open-ended schedule designed to ascertain organization structure, policies, informal style, and history. These interviews were supplemented with agency records, documents, and statistics provided by each department.

Variables

To evaluate the impact of department strategies on officer knowledge, a dichotomous measure of officer awareness of citizen organizations was devised. Officers able to name one or more citizen groups operating in the neighborhood were categorized as knowledgeable; officers unable to name any groups were considered unknowledgeable. Respondents were asked to specify by name any groups conducting volunteer patrols, crime prevention, or police-community relations in their respective beats. An officer's ability to name a group does not reflect the degree or nature of his or her involvement with the group, but it does indicate at least an awareness of a potential source for developing knowledge of how people in the neighborhood think and feel about police-related problems. Of the 888 respondents without missing values on an independent variable, 38.5 percent could name at least one citizen organization active in the neighborhood.

The impact of several organizational arrangements and neighborhood characteristics on officers' knowledge was estimated in a discriminant analysis. Discriminant analysis allows the analyst to estimate the independent effects of explanatory variables on a categorical dependent variable while simultaneously controlling for the effects of each independent variable on the dependent variable (Klecka, 1980). Discriminant analysis seeks the linear combination of independent variables that best distinguishes the groups of a categorical dependent variable. The following "discriminating" variables were used in the statistical analysis:

Organizational Arrangements

Population of the department's patrol jurisdiction

Population of the primary assignment area (PAA) of the officer's beat—a measure of the stability of beat assignments

Years the officer had lived in the jurisdiction

Years of experience as a police officer

Racial match between the officer and the neighborhood

Proportion of patrol work time not assigned by department

Control Variables

Visibility of citizen organizations in each neighborhood

Median family income of neighborhood residents

Level of violent victimization in the neighborhood

The first two variables are indicators of organizational structure. Patrol jurisdiction populations are highly correlated with department size and are listed in Table 2.1. The population of the primary assignment area (PAA) is a measure of the scale of patrol decentralization/centralization for each neighborhood. The PAA is determined by the beat or beats in which officers routinely serving a study neighborhood work in a year. The boundaries for the PAA relevant to each study neighborhood were determined by officers' roll call assignments (based on department records) and where they actually spent their time on patrol (based on in-person observations). There is one PAA associated with each study neighborhood. The size of the PAA is indicated by the residential population within its boundaries. PAA populations are as small as 5,600, reflecting a highly decentralized, neighborhood policing structure. The largest PAA is 209,700 (the population of a county sheriff's entire patrol jurisdiction), indicating a rotating, highly centralized beat assignment practice. In this sample, small PAAs are found in several small municipalities and a few large cities. The PAA population is a contextual variable associated with the neighborhood about which each officer was interviewed.[3]

The next three variables represent the consequences of several personnel practices in the study departments. The length of each officer's residency in the jurisdiction allows inferences about the underlying assumption of residency requirements—that residence in the jurisdiction increases officers' attachments to the community. The length of residency in the jurisdiction served by the officer's department ranges from 0 to over 20 years, the average being 12.3. The number of years of police experience for each respondent reflects the department's officer-retention capabilities. Police experience in this sample ranged from a few months to over 20 years, but the majority had served fewer than 5 years. The sample average was 5.1 and the standard deviation was 4. Knowing the racial match between officers and the residents on their beats allows inferences about the effects of various officer assignment strategies. In this sample the vast majority of officers (518) were white, serving white neighborhoods; 172 were white, serving black neighborhoods; 113 were white in racially mixed neighborhoods. Of the 85 black officers in the sample, 52 served black neighborhoods, 21 served white neighborhoods, and 12 served racially mixed neighborhoods.[4]

One variable reflects operational policies and practices affecting the demands placed on patrol officers' time by the department's dispatchers, supervisors, and administrative requirements. Where there is considerable pressure to handle dispatched calls, complete reports, and conduct other administrative tasks, less time is available for developing beat contacts and expanding one's knowledge base. Of course, making "free" or unassigned time available to the officer (by manipulating the ratio of manpower to expected demand) does not ensure that officers will use it to expand their knowledge. In fact, they may use this time to avoid contact with the public. The amount of unassigned time available to an officer will vary considerably according to the shift he or she works, the day of the week, the time of year, and many other unpredictable factors affecting the public's demand for service. Nevertheless, fairly consistent patterns of demand do emerge over time, so that some estimate of the availability of unassigned time can be made. Observations of the subsample of respondents accompanied by researchers while on patrol provide a rough estimate of the average amount of unassigned time available to officers serving each beat. Based on observation of 15 shifts per neighborhood, the amount of unassigned patrol time varies from 42-83 percent, the average being 65 and the standard deviation being 9.

The visibility of citizen organizations in each neighborhood is a key control variable that may be responsive to departmental community development programs aimed at neighborhood organizations. The level of citizen organization activity is a direct function of the choices of its membership and the awareness of residents of these activities. To the extent that departments promote such organizations, however, they improve the likelihood that both the public and patrol officers will be aware of them. Where citizen organization visibility is low, one would not expect officer awareness to be as widespread as areas where visibility is high. Interviews with citizen organization leaders in the study jurisdiction suggested varying levels of activity. An indirect indicator of their activity and a direct indicator of their visibility is the proportion of residents able to name citizen organizations in their neighborhoods. This is a contextual variable associated with the neighborhood served by each officer. This ranged from 4 to 55 percent. In 36 of the neighborhoods, fewer than 15 percent of the resident respondents were aware of a citizen organization active in their neighborhood.

Two other neighborhood characteristics were used as control variables: the wealth of residents and the level of violent crime. Low-income areas present more obstacles to officer involvement with the community, since officers tend not to identify personally with the poor. However, high violence in a neighborhood poses a threat to the officer's safety as well as other citizens and is, therefore, expected to encourage officers to become familiar with potentially supporting neighborhood institutions. Neighborhood wealth and violence were estimated from responses to the residential surveys. The median family income for neighborhoods ranged from $4,300 to $22,300. The level of annual violent victimization ranged from 0 to 43 per thousand residents.

Results

Table 2.2 shows the results of the discriminant analysis. The first two columns show the mean value of responses for the knowledgeable and unknowledgeable officers. However, comparison of group means does not allow an assessment of the separate impact of each explanatory variable, controlling for the effects of all others. The standardized canonical discriminant function coefficient in the last column represents the contribution of each variable to the discriminating ability of the linear model relative to all other variables in the model. Its interpretation is similar to the standardized regression coefficient (Beta) in the interpretation of multiple regression models (Klecka, 1980: 29).

Patrol jurisdiction population and PAA population show the expected inverse relationship to officer knowledge. The following variables show a direct relationship to officer knowledge: years resided in the jurisdiction, years of police experience, visibility of citizen organizations to residents, neighborhood wealth, and level of neighborhood violence.

The strongest effects of the racial matching are shown in the nature of the neighborhood, not the officer. Serving in a black neighborhood, whether the officer is white or black tends to increase the probability of officer awareness (to roughly the same extent). Regardless of race, an officer serving a racially mixed neighborhood is predicted to be only slightly less likely to be knowledgeable than a white officer serving a white neighborhood (the reference category). The coefficient for the black officer in a white neighborhood is similarly negligible. Thus, it is not the interaction of individual officer race and neighborhood race that shows consequences in these data—only the neighborhood's racial profile. When officer and neighborhood race are separated as two variables in the model, the coefficients are respectively −.08 and .27, all other coefficients remaining essentially unchanged. Officers are most likely to be aware of citizen organizations if they serve black neighborhoods and less likely in white and mixed neighborhoods.

The availability of unassigned time is inversely related to officer knowledge. Those officers serving neighborhoods with patterns of high demand on their time are most likely to be knowledgeable. This suggests that giving officers large amounts of undirected discretionary time is less conducive to developing beat awareness than keeping officers busy answering calls for service.

The visibility of citizen organizations in the neighborhood and the availability of unassigned patrol time contribute the most to the model's ability to distinguish knowledgeable and unknowledgeable officers (.52

TABLE 2.2 Group Means and Standardized Discriminant Function Coefficients

Independent Variable	Officers with Knowledge	Officers without Knowledge	Standard Coefficient
(N)	(546)	(342)	
Patrol jurisdiction population	230,242	203,694	-.36
PAA population	47,328	79,761	-.26
Years lived in jurisdiction	14.0	11.2	.20
Years served as police officer	5.8	4.7	.27
White officer in white nbhd	.52	.62	*
Black officer in white nbhd	.01	.03	-.16
White officer in mixed nbhd	.14	.12	-.09
Black officer in mixed nbhd	.01	.01	-.09
White officer in black nbhd	.21	.18	.26
Black officer in black nbhd	.10	.03	.21
% patrol time unassigned	61.0	65.7	-.48
% knowledgeable residents	16.9	11.3	.52
Median family income of nbhd	11,272	11,164	.33
Violent victimizations/1000 res.	11.9	8.7	.27

*Reference category.

59

and $-.48$, respectively). The predictive power of each is about twice that of PAA population, for example. The coefficients for size of patrol jurisdiction and PAA, years of residence in the jurisdiction, years of police experience, neighborhood racial profile, neighborhood wealth, and neighborhood violence are between .19 and .36 magnitude.

The overall ability of this model to discriminate between the two groups of officers is moderate. The discriminant function defined by this model correctly classifies 70 percent of the officers, which is 20 percent more than would be correctly classified by random assignment. A standardized measure of the proportional reduction in error from random assignment is given by tau, which is .4 for this model (266 actual errors as opposed to 444 expected by chance).

CONCLUSIONS

The results of this analysis are not particularly encouraging for those who believe that a patrol officer's knowledge of his or her beat is an important part of performance. Of every 10 officers surveyed, 6 were unable to name even one citizen organization active in crime or police problems on their beats. Furthermore, the ability of a variety of organizational arrangements subject to government manipulation was modest. The analysis suggests that many of the reforms advocated in the 1960s and 1970s are by themselves unlikely to have a substantial impact on police awareness of citizen organizations. Keeping police services decentralized (by not consolidating small departments and by stabilizing beat assignments) would seem to improve the probability of officer awareness of the beat, but not to a great extent. Trying to retain experienced officers and requiring residency in the jurisdiction do not show great promise either. Based on this analysis, the most effective way for administrators to facilitate officer awareness of citizen organizations is to ensure that they have as much contact as possible with the public and encourage voluntary citizen organizations to increase their visibility in their neighborhoods.

This analysis is not the ultimate test of a department's capacity to increase beat knowledge, however. With the possible exception of two neighborhoods in St. Louis, none of the departments had committed substantial resources to a program specifically designed to increase street-level officers' contact with community organizations.[5] This suggests that extraordinary efforts such as San Diego's may be necessary to make large gains in patrol officers' knowledge of citizen organizations. Departments must ensure that officers make the effort to learn more about the community they serve. This can be done in routine service contacts with the public, but it will also require that departments direct their officers to spend more of their free time getting to know people and organizations on their beats. Under these circumstances, they are less pressed with the necessity of taking immediate action and can pay more attention to learning about the people with whom they deal. The substantial amounts of unassigned time available to officers in even the busiest beats in this sample indicate that a patrol operation directed this way need not degrade the capacity of departments to respond to demands for service. Given the lack of evidence that officer isolation strategies (such as preventive patrol) produce any beneficial results (Kelling, 1978), the San Diego project seems worthy of emulation.

The limitations of the measure of beat knowledge employed in this and other research have been discussed earlier. Improvement in measuring beat knowledge is possible, although it requires a much different approach to information collection and dissemination than usually displayed in police departments. Providing statistical summaries of neighborhoods and lists of service agencies and neighborhood organizations is only the beginning. To predict events on the beat and to evaluate someone's ability to predict events requires an extensive knowledge base peculiar to each beat. Departments can use their patrol officers to develop neighborhood histories from their own experiences. For example, officers could share their experiences on juvenile gangs to obtain some estimation of their propensity to cause trouble. Because officers' different patrol styles inevitably produce different and sometimes conflicting information, it is essential that departments set aside time for officers to share and discuss their information. Over time, a knowledge base for each beat could be compiled by the officers who have worked it, and this would serve as a source for assessing the knowledge level of those newly assigned to the beat. It would provide a standard for formally assessing beat knowledge, and it could serve as a reference for discussion when new information is added with continual updating. Discussion is particularly important for developing the understanding component of beat knowledge. The accuracy of an understanding of a particular problem is not verifiable in the sense that one can verify judgment that predicts the event. Police supervisors and managers may want to monitor their officers' understanding of problems to compare the extent to which their officers' understanding comports with the understanding *they* wish to promote.

Unless carefully implemented and administered, such a program could produce officially sanctioned "bull" sessions for swapping yarns. Overcoming police reluctance to share information and ideas will not be easy. Several ethnographies offer graphic examples of the jealousy with which officers guard personal information about their beats, and a recent quantitative study suggests that there is currently not a strong association between police officers' communication with each other about their work and satisfaction with their jobs (Dunning and Hochstedler, 1982). To the extent that such relationships exist, they are strongest with upward communication rather than horizontal communication within the agency, which would be expected under the current structure of police agency incentives to share information.

The necessary organizational changes appear to be profound, but by committing the organization to this type of performance program, administrators will be able to assess the ability of individuals and the organization to achieve a crucial intervening factor between organizational inputs and the achievement of ultimate goals. Greater knowledge of the beat is a necessary if not sufficient condition for improving what police do. Governing is the principal function of the police officer, and knowledge of the governed is essential for progress toward a safe community and fairer, more caring police.

NOTES

1. The Police Services Study was a joint project of Indiana University and the University of North Carolina. The project was funded by the National Science Foundation, Division of Applied Research under Grant NSF GI-43949.

2. Boundaries were adjusted in some instances to increase socioeconomic homogeneity and to accommodate changes in beat designation according to the time of day. In some of the smallest communities, the entire jurisdiction comprised the neighborhood. Neighborhood populations ranged from 3,500 to 22,000, most falling within the 5,000-15,000 range. Seven neighborhoods were considered poverty level ($4,000-6,000 median family income) and were black (75 percent or more). Of the 33 neighborhoods in the low income range ($6,000-14,000 median family income), 7 were black, 9 were racially mixed (25-75 percent black), and 17 were white (less than 25 percent black). Eleven of the 13 middle income neighborhoods ($14,000-18,000 median family income) were white, one was racially mixed, and one was black. All 7 upper middle income neighborhoods ($18,000-23,000 median family income) were white.

3. See Mastrofski (1981a, 1981b) for details on this indicator. Actual location in or outside the officers' assigned beats was determined by in-person observation for a matched sample of 15 shifts in each study neighborhood. PAAs used in this analysis refer to beats that (1) accounted for at least 75 percent of the work assignments of

the officers who served them, and (2) accounted for 70 percent of the observed officers' citizen encounters and time on mobile patrol.

4. The racial match was entered as a series of dummy variables for each of the six possibilities, using white officers in white neighborhoods as the reference group.

5. The St. Louis department made a special effort to give officers a chance to meet citizen organizations and share beat information through an experimental team policing program. Taking this into account in the statistical model had no significant effects on the model's ability to discriminate officers correctly between groups and on the values of the coefficients of the other variables. This lack of effect may be due to the deterioration of this part of the team policing program, noted by team officers and research personnel on site. Demands for response to calls for service reportedly cut into time set aside for team meetings and community organization work.

REFERENCES

BOYDSTUN, J. E. and M. E. SHERRY (1975) San Diego Community Profile: Final Report. Washington, DC: Police Foundation.

BROWN, M. K. (1981) Working the Street: Police Discretion and the Dilemmas of Reform. New York: Russell Sage Foundation.

COOPER, J. L. (1980) The Police and the Ghetto. Port Washington, NY: Kennikat Press.

DAVIS, E. M. (1978) Staff One: A Perspective on Effective Police Management. Englewood Cliffs, NJ: Prentice-Hall.

DUNNING, C. M. and E. HOCHSTEDLER (1982) "Satisfaction with communication in a police organization: 'shooting the shit,' 'horsenecking,' and 'brownie' reports," in J. R. Greene (ed.) Managing Police Work: Issues and Analysis. Beverly Hills: Sage.

GAY, W. G., J. P. WOODWARD, H. T. DAY, J. P. O'NEIL, and C. J. TUCKER (1977) Issues in Team Policing: A Review of the Literature. Washington, DC: U.S. Government Printing Office.

GOLDSTEIN, H. (1977) Policing a Free Society. Cambridge, MA: Ballinger.

JACOBS, J. B. and J. COHEN (1978) "The impact of racial integration on the police." Journal of Police Science and Administration 6: 168-183.

KELLING, G. L. (1978) "Police field services and crime: the presumed effects of a capacity." Crime and Delinquency (April): 173-184.

KLECKA, W. R. (1980) "Discriminant analysis." Quantitative Applications in the Social Sciences 07-019. Beverly Hills, CA: Sage.

MASTROFSKI, S. (1981a) "Policing the beat: the impact of organizational scale on patrol officer behavior in urban residential neighborhoods." Journal of Criminal Justice 9: 343-358.

――― (1981b) "Reforming police: the impact of patrol assignment patterns on officer behavior in urban residential neighborhoods." Doctoral dissertation, University of North Carolina at Chapel Hill.

MENKE, B. A., M. F. WHITE, and W. L. CAREY (1982) "Police professionalism: pursuit of excellence or political power?" in J. R. Greene (ed.) Managing Police Work: Issues and Analysis. Beverly Hills: Sage.

MUIR, W. K., Jr. (1977) Police: Streetcorner Politicians. Chicago: University of Chicago Press.

MURPHY, P. V. and T. PLATE (1977) Commissioner. New York: Simon & Schuster.

MYREN, R. A. (1972) "Decentralization and citizen participation in criminal justice systems." Public Administration Review (October): 718-738.

PARKS, R. B. (1980) "Using sample surveys to compare police performance." Bloomington: Workshop in Political Theory and Policy Analysis, Indiana University.

POMERLEAU, D. D. (1982) "Crime prevention and the community," in B. L. Garmire (ed.) Local Government Police Management (2nd ed.). Washington, DC: International City Management Association.

PROTTAS, J. (1978) "The power of the street-level bureaucrat in public service bureaucracies." Urban Affairs Quarterly 13: 285-312.

RUBINSTEIN, J. (1973) City Police. New York: Garrar, Straus & Giroux.

SCHMANDT, H. J. (1972) "Municipal decentralization: an overview." Public Administration Review (October): 571-588.

SCHWARTZ, A. I. and S. N. CLARREN (1978) The Cincinnati Team Policing Experiment: A Technical Report. Washington, DC: Police Foundation.

SHARP, E. B. (1978) "Citizen organizations and participation in law enforcement advocacy and coproduction: the role of incentives." Doctoral dissertation, University of North Carolina at Chapel Hill.

VAN MAANEN, J. (1974) "Working the street: a developmental view of police behavior," in H. Jacob (ed.) The Potential for Reform of Criminal Justice. Beverly Hills: Sage.

WAMBAUGH, J. (1972) The Blue Knight. Boston: Little, Brown.

WHITAKER, G. P., S. MASTROFSKI, E. OSTROM, R. B. PARKS, and S. L. PERCY (1980) Measuring Police Agency Performance. Report to the National Institute of Justice. Chapel Hill: University of North Carolina.

WILSON, J. Q. and G. L. KELLING (1982) "The police and neighborhood safety: broken windows." Atlantic Monthly (March): 29-38.

WILSON, O. W. (1963) Police Administration (2nd ed.). New York: McGraw-Hill.

WYCOFF, M. A. (1982) "Improving police performance measurement: one more voice." Urban Interest 4: 8-16.

3.

JUDGING POLICE PERFORMANCE:
Views and Behavior of Patrol Officers

David N. Allen
Pennsylvania State University
Michael G. Maxfield
Indiana University

The police performance literature has been growing rapidly, and theoretical approaches to examining the topic are beginning to be defined in a clearer manner. To date, however, no research has been conducted that connects the emphasis supervisors (sergeants and lieutenants) place on certain performance dimensions and actual police officer behavior along those performance dimensions.

This work represents an initial attempt to link the performance expectation that street supervisors have about their patrol officers to patrol officer behavior. Individual officer performance is primarily viewed as arrests, even though considerable problems are evident in an emphasis on arrests (Parks, 1975; Ricco and Heaphy, 1977; Sherman and Glick, 1980; Skogan and Antunes, 1979). The element of supervision is brought into the discussion in order to portray how officers receive information about what is expected of them in terms of performance. Contrasting approaches to street supervision are posed and different outcomes are suggested as

Authors' Note: *The authors wish to thank several people for invaluable assistance in this project. George Antunes and Monica Wheatly contributed countless hours of voluntary labor collecting data. Thomas Scheutchuck, Christine Gault, Daniel Kennedy, and Frank Christello also assisted in data collection, coding, and computer operations. We are indebted to all officers in the Louisville Police Department for*

resulting from these approaches. Analysis of 150 patrol officers and their supervisors leads to conclusions about performance and the role supervision plays in directing patrol-officer behavior.

PERFORMANCE MEASUREMENT:
A METHODOLOGICAL MORASS

Police agencies are purposeful organizations. Although many would like to see the police function better defined, such as a stated preference for crime fighting over assistance to individuals, one can still contend that police activities are directed toward desired purposes. As such, police agencies need to determine how well individuals are meeting intended purposes.

In a well-functioning police agency, individual activity at all levels of the hierarchy is directed to the organization's intended purposes. Matching individuals' rational self-interests with the agencies' purpose is one of the most difficult but necessary tasks of management (Downs, 1967). Such a matching is accomplished through a structure of incentives that act as work prescriptions. Unfortunately, this logic of performance is not present in most police agencies.

Police agencies exist in an environment that inhibits direction of the individual's activities. Confusion about intended purposes is characteristic of policing.[1] Identification of relevant publics is difficult given the vast percentage of officers' time spent with the distressed or the victims of crime and actual (or perceived) victimizers, and not with "average" citizens. Officers have many conflicting demands; they often find themselves having to satisfy the contradictory preferences of superiors and the com-

their cooperation. In particular, Sergeant John Ansman, Lieutenant Fred Rogers, Major Sherman Anderson, and Officer Robert Bauer actively supported the project and helped us over numerous hurdles. Michael Bewley and Ron Pregliasco, of the Louisville-Jefferson County Criminal Justice Commission, were also particularly helpful. This project was supported in part by a Project Fund grant from the School of Public and Environmental Affairs, Indiana University. Office space in Louisville was graciously provided by the Department of Political Science, University of Louisville. The vast majority of the time spent collecting data for this project was contributed by the authors and the persons named above. The authors note that any findings, views, and opinions presented herein are those of the authors and should not be construed as representative of the Louisville Department of Police, Indiana University, or Pennsylvania State University.

munity (Perry and Sornoff, 1973). Managers, especially first-line supervisors, face problems in directing officer behavior given the few positive inducements available to get officers to work. Most of the incentives at a supervisor's disposal are negative, such as imposing time off from work without pay (Brown, 1981). A few police scholars have observed that the patrol supervisor's ability to issue orders, as well as remain in the position as the squad's supervisor, are largely based on officer goodwill (Rubinstein, 1973: 59; Van Maanen, 1974: 115). Add to this dismal list of management constraints such factors as individualistic police officer personality characteristics (Rhead et al., 1968; Lefkowiz, 1975), fixed-salary union contracts (Prottas, 1978), imprecise measurement tools, and budgetary retrenchment, and it is not difficult to see why performance measurement is in such an intellectual quandary.

One way to point out some methodological problems of performance measurement[2] is to examine some of the general trends in the literature. This brief overview is not meant to be an exhaustive treatise on the topic; rather, its purpose is to provide evidence for the assertion that individual performance measurement has some unifying concepts and techniques but that many fundamental problems still exist (Stevens and McDavid, 1981).

The Common Call for Multiple Indicators

Police have multiple purposes and provide services to different publics that have different interests. In the literature of performance assessment it is common to see the case for multiple indicators advanced (Marx, 1978; Ostrom, 1973; Parks, 1975). Emphasis on one indicator or one set of common indicators may lead to faulty conclusions about performance.[3] Skolnick (1966) advances the notion that by focusing on one criterion of performance, clearance rates, suboptimization occurs in regard to other critieria. For example, Skolnick contends that the incentives for promotion and workload reduction are so designed that investigators often have suspected that habitual burglars confess to many crimes in order to have an excessive backlog of cases cleared. Through the offer of reduced charges, most burglars accept the bargain and confess to a number of burglaries. Outstanding case investigations are closed, while the real burglar is at large and no property is recovered. In this example, the indicators are internally generated (arrests) and internally controlled (offers of reduced charges). Another complication in performance measurement arises from externally controlled factors.

Problems with Internally Generated, Externally Controlled Indicators

It is common to find in the literature references to the inappropriateness of judging police performance on factors over which the police have only partial control (Parks, 1975; Repetto, 1980). Lack of control is typical of internally generated indicators such as crime rate.[4] Estimates have been made that from 50 to 70 percent of the crimes in some major categories are not even reported to police (Skogan, 1976). Conviction rates are an example of an agency (internally) generated performance indicator dependent on external control. A conviction is dependent on more than a good "clean" arrest for a clear violation of the law. Arrests may be dismissed if the prosecuting attorney's office does not have the personnel, investigative capability, or desire to bring the case to court. Similarly, plea bargaining is seen as a useful, albeit undesirable, way to decrease excessive court backlog and/or achieve higher conviction rates (Wice, 1978).

The Inadequacy of Supervisor Rating of Officers

Recently, attention has been given to the role of supervisors in officer performance evaluation. Sharp (1982: 40) contends that supervisor evaluation "is a form of data that is relevant and believable to police practitioners themselves." Her work, however, seems to ignore a prevalent conclusion by two social scientists that such type of performance evaluation has not kept pace with the changing nature of police work (Farr and Landy, 1979: 61).

The methodological problems associated with supervisor-based assessment (Jacobs, 1981) have led some to question the worth of performance evaluations. In her evaluation of measurement systems, Nadel (1978: 43) stated that "evaluations have a limited significance." Such a finding is replicated by Kohlan (1973: 170) in his evaluation of promotional procedures in fifteen jurisdictions:

> ... it appears that the typical performance evaluation contributes little to the total selection process. Since almost every one is rated "above-average" (despite efforts to persuade the raters to use a wider range of ratings), the performance evaluation has little discriminating power. In practice, it is nearly the same as adding a constant to every candidate's score.

Our research in Louisville leads us to similar conclusions. We have reported elsewhere (Maxfield et al., 1981: 28):

> ... sergeants and lieutenants [were asked] what impact they felt annual performance ratings had on an officer's career, whether they were critically important, routinely filed and forgotten, or somewhere between these two extremes. Few labor under the illusion that their judgments are critical to an officer's career. Only 14 percent of sergeants and 18 percent of lieutenants attached such weight to their ratings. . . . Few officers are rated lower than 95 on a scale ranging from zero to 100. Such uniformly high ratings were totally discrepant with our perception of average performance, and with most officer's perception of their fellow workers.

The result of factors such as the operational failure of "standardized" performance assessment, problems of external influences on agency-generated indicators, divergent multiple indicators, and a general lack of theory-based direction for indicator development has been a reliance on two predominent, easily obtained indicators: arrests and citations. One author has stated that "currently in the city concerned, productivity has been operationally defined by the police department as arrests and summonses" (Nadel, 1978:39).

Arrests as a Performance Measure:
Of Questionable Worth

It is widely acknowledged that arrests and citations are easily quantified, but the quality of such measures is highly suspect. These measures are highly regarded by supervisors in their assessments of officers, and the availability of such information affords us an opportunity to conduct an in-depth examination of factors affecting one of these quantity type indicators: arrests.

Arrests are frequently perceived as having a central role in both crime control and order maintenance (Bittner, 1970; LaFave, 1965). The crime control role is straightforward, while the order maintenance role is somewhat problematic. Arrests as order maintenance:

> are often used to maintain the image of full enforcement of the law; to detain, harass, or punish persons "known" to be offensive,

deviant or in violation of laws; and to extend control over hostile situations or persons [Hepburn, 1981: 96].

It is also possible that the high value an officer places on an arrest could lead to an officer letting a problem continue or develop to the point where an arrest is warranted, even though control over the situation could have been achieved at an earlier point (Jones, 1980). Such a situation is clearly detrimental to order maintenance. Arrests are also though to have a negative effect on other aspects of policing, especially service or social welfare roles (Jones, 1980; Nadel, 1978).

Although many have discussed the problems associated with using arrests as performance indicators (Parks, 1975; Ricco and Heaphy, 1977; Sherman and Glick, 1980; Skogan and Antunes, 1979), arrests seem to have become an end in themselves. Perhaps this fact of policing is best explained by Jones (1980: 64) in his discussion of British police behavior:

> You cannot possibly recommend a police officer for a specialist department by saying 'This man has potential because he is of sound character, he's well balanced. I've had long conversations with this man and he obviously appreciates the role of police constable in society, etc.' No, you can't say that; what you can say is this man has had seventy-five prisoners for crime.

THE COMMAND AND BARGAINING
MODELS OF SUPERVISION

Police organizations are structured along the lines of classical bureaucracies. Rigid centralized control, as seen in the quasi-military police structure, is believed to engender a high degree of supervisory control. Multiple layers of hierarchy, interconnected by the unity of command principle, supposedly provide excellent channels for information transfer. Information about street conditions and possible alternative policing strategies moves from the bottom to the top, and subsequent policy adjustments move back down from the top to the bottom.

The style of supervision in the classical bureaucratic police organization has been characterized as the command model (Maxfield et al., 1981). The command model of supervision assumes a high degree of officer subordination to supervisors, based in part on the legitimate authority of hierarchical superiors to issue orders and officers willingness to follow orders. A high degree of predictability is assumed to be the result of rule-guided behavior in a stable, spatially uniform task environment (Allen, 1982). The classic bureaucratic organization, and in this case the typical policy agency, operates on the implicit assumption that the individuals who work within it share similar notions concerning intended purposes and outcomes of policing.

A contrasting perspective on supervisory practices is apparent in the observational studies of police that point to the inherent limits of the command model (Maxfield et al., 1981). The contrasting perspective, called the bargaining model, adheres to the notion that police officers are appreciably independent from supervisory control. Officers are typified as behaving in a highly individualistic discretionary manner. Supervisory oversight of officers is minimal, given the spatial dispersion inherent in patrol operations and officers' beliefs that their training and experience, that is, their professionalism, gives them the requisite ability to handle nearly all situations they encounter. The desire of officers not to be second-guessed by supervisors is evident in an earlier reported finding:

> When asked what action they would prefer a supervisor to take when present at their runs, 76 percent of the 152 officers we interviewed responded that they expected the supervisor to back them up like another patrol officer. Only 10 percent of officers said they would expect some form of guidance from their supervisors, and 13 percent preferred the sergeant to "do nothing" at the scene of encounters [Maxfield et al., 1981: 24-25].

Information flows, as viewed from this nontraditional perspective, are not uniform and precise along hierarchical lines of authority. Rather, information is viewed as distorted and tasks become redefined to fit the personal self-interests of those assigned to execute the directives (Allen, 1982). Because individual behavior is guided by rational self-interest, no assumptions are made concerning shared intended purposes. Work is guided by the individual officers' sense of appropriate behavior and the existing, albeit inadequate, incentive structure. Supervisors, unable to induce preferred behavior with negatively oriented incentives (such as days off without pay), work with their few positive inducements to obtain desired outcomes. The lack of positive inducements is evident in the way the Louisville Police Department supervisors occasionally devised reward schemes (such as dismissing officers a few hours early on the late evening shift) when the officers caught a burglar in a house or uncovered evidence that broke a string of unsolved cases. This special reward activity is openly acknowledged to be a violation of departmental rules, but, due to the results it engenders, it is benignly ignored by upper-level commanders.

Not all officers respond to the same inducements. Younger, upwardly aspiring officers may respond to a different set of rewards than "short-timing" veterans. For example, a young officer may want a fast-track beat to provide ample opportunity for making arrests, while the older officer may want a slower beat where police presence may be all the community needs to assure safety and security.

To date, our research has only begun to address the direct verification of the bargaining model approach to supervision. Previous research, however, has provided evidence that tends strongly to refute the validity of the command model. In particular, Allen (1979, 1982) has shown that under some circumstances supervision has a positive, though weak, effect on officer activities at encounter scenes and shift level officer outputs. The primary explanation of such findings concern the constraints that supervisors face in directing work on the street. In particular, emphasis has been placed on the supervisor's lack of reward power.[5] Another plausible explanation for the negligible control supervisors exhibit concerns different priorities of work, a focus of this analysis. In this chapter we address this issue of work priorities and other concerns considered earlier, by considering the following questions:

- What performance indicators do patrol supervisors deem important?

- How do officers perceive the appropriateness of their supervisors' indicators?

- How do the supervisors indicators affect officer beliefs about their work?

- Is there a relationship between supervisor emphasis on quantity of work measures and higher levels of quantity type work by patrol officers?

RESEARCH SETTING

In order to address issues concerning performance assessment, we collected data in a police department of a moderately large city. Louisville, Kentucky, was selected as the site, largely for reasons of convenience and the fact that officials in the police department at all levels were cooperative in granting us access for the study. The Louisville Police Department is not meant to be portrayed as a typical or atypical urban police department. The findings only relate to the department as it existed during the period of field research, the summer of 1981. Several administrative and personnel changes in the department have occurred since the data were collected, although none of the changes is in any way connected to this study.

Patrol officers and supervisors in five of the six districts rotate shifts every 28 days. The remaining district assigns general patrol personnel to permanent shifts. In all six districts patrol officers and supervisors are on permanent platoon assignments, remaining together as a unit whether or not shift assignments are rotated. Most patrol officers in a platoon are permanently assigned to a specific beat within a district. With few exceptions, all beat patrol units are allocated two officers per car, although short-term personnel shortages and regular days off require that some officers ride alone.

We were interested only in supervisory practices for general area patrol. No attempt was made to examine tactical, traffic, and criminal investigation supervisory practices.

DATA COLLECTION

Approximately one year prior to the summer of 1981, the authors and several students rode with supervisors in Louisville to become more familiar with supervisory practices. These preliminary observations and lengthy informal conversations with supervisors and patrol officers guided the construction of questionnaires and plans for collecting other data.

At an introductory meeting with a district commander, we discussed the purpose of the study and sought the cooperation of each captain to facilitate interviews and other data collection activities. Difficulties in scheduling an interview with one of the six district commanders precluded any further data collection in that district. After we discussed the purpose of the study with a district commander, we arranged for at least one member of our research team to begin interviewing supervisors and officers in each of the three regular platoons in that district. Before roll call, we met with the lieutenant or sergeant assigned to each platoon and explained our procedures: that we wanted to interview both supervisors and all the patrol officers on permanent assignment who had been with the platoon for at least six months. A few skeptical supervisors were not uncooperative to the point of denying us access to their platoons, but two refused to be interviewed. Due to the two refusals, two supervisors who were unavailable because of sick leave or vacation, and one who had recently retired and had not yet been replaced, we were able in 10 of the 15 platoons studied to interview both the sergeant and the lieutenant. A total of 14 sergeants and 11 lieutenants were interviewed.

After our personal interviews with each supervisor, we requested that units be sent to the station one at a time for interviewing. By making return trips whenever we had been unable to interview all patrol officers during the initial session, we were able to complete interviews with 152 officers. No interviews were refused by patrol officers. All interviews were conducted in a setting, such as a private room or a secluded area, away from others at the station. The officer interview schedule covered many of the same questions that were asked of their supervisors. Often the questions on the two surveys were changed to address similar issues from the supervisor or patrol officer point of view. Arrest data are also used in this analysis. These data were obtained from departmental records. Because the focus of this analysis is on quantity of work performance indicators, no attempt has been made to categorize arrests by type or seriousness of the offense. Subsequent analysis will examine other performance indicators, but such examination is beyond the scope of this presentation.

FINDINGS

Officers were asked to state the indicators that their direct supervisors used to evaluate their performance. From the numerous responses given to this question we were able to create six mutually exclusive, exhaustive codes.[6] The officers were permitted to give up to five different responses. We have no reason to believe that the first mention is any more important than any other mention or that a greater number of mentions is any more important than a lesser number of mentions. Some supervisors stress more than one indicator; therefore we expect that some officers will respond with more than one mention.

The first indicator, quantity of work, is rather straightforward. Whenever specific mentions such as "arrests," "citations," "warrants served," or general statements such as "statistics" or "activity" were given, the quantity of work code applies. Work characteristics/habits refer to both desirable and undesirable approaches or orientations officers take to their work. For example, statements such as "late to work," "dealing with the public," "drinking" or "sleeping on the job," and "good knowledge of the beat" were coded as work characteristics/habits. The third category refers to quality of work. Some responses that fit into this category are "arrests that lead to conviction" and "good felony arrests." Quality of paperwork is the fourth category. Some statements that were coded into this category are "how well reports are filled out" and "how often reports have to be redone." The fifth category concerns personal and psychological character-istics. Both desirable and undesirable orientations were included in this code. Some typical statements were "good judgment," "physical appear-ance," "bad temper," and "poor attitude." The sixth category of indica-tors is labeled "desire to do work." Frequent statements in this category were "frequently arrives first at the scene," "generates own work," and "avoids work whenever possible."

The aforementioned six codes are used for both the supervisor and officer statements of indicators that are stressed. For the supervisor data, one additional code is used. This code refers to civil service criteria for evaluation. One supervisor said that he stresses each of the civil service items equally. The "don't know" response was nonexistent for supervisors and very low for officers. Because of its low frequency it was treated as missing data.

The most frequently mentioned response by officers was supervisor emphasis on quantity of work (Table 3.1).[7] Nearly 62 percent of the officers mentioned this. Slightly over half the officers mentioned work characteristics/habits. Quality of work was mentioned by about 42 percent of the officers. The least mentioned indicator was quality of paperwork, 17.4 percent.

Officers were asked if they thought the indicators their direct super-visors stress are good ways to judge performance. The majority, 67.8 percent, believe that supervisors do use good performance indicators. Frequently, those who said the supervisors' indicators were good also qualified their answer to say that whether or not they are good or is a lesser issue than the question of whether supervisors stress the best indicators of those available. Officers who said their supervisors do not use good indicators frequently said that it is not possible to evaluate accu-rately the performance of a police officer.

One way to examine whether officers have an understanding of the supervisor's performance expectations is to assess the similarity of percep-tions concerning performance. By asking supervisors what indicators they stressed and asking officers what indicators they believe their supervisors stress, we are able to gauge similarity of perceptions. Our data are based on all five districts. It is important to note that we were able to interview

TABLE 3.1   Supervisor's Emphasized Indicators by Whether Officer
             Percieves Them as Appropriate

Officer's Belief About Indicators Supervisor Emphasizes	Frequency Col %	Supervisors Use Good Indicators	Supervisors do Not Use Good Indicators	Row Total
Quality of Work		54	38	92
		53.5	79.2	61.7
Work characteristics/ habits		58	17	75
		57.4	35.4	50.3
Quality of Work		53	10	63
		52.5	20.8	42.3
Quality of paperwork		19	7	26
		18.8	14.6	17.4
Personnel or psychological characteristics		48	13	61
		47.5	27.1	40.9
Desire to do work		43	10	53
		42.6	20.8	35.6
Column total		101	48	
		67.8	32.2	N = 149

both the sergeant and lieutenant in only 10 of the 15 platoons. In separate analyses of only those 10 platoons it was found that neither the sergeant nor the lieutenant in each platoon mentioned the same indicators.

Generally, one sees some variation between supervisors and officers among the five districts, but for the entire department the variation is considerably lower (Table 3.2). We set an arbitrary 25 percent difference between supervisors and officers to determine similarity of performance indicators. Based on that criterion, the two groups are roughly similar on all but two characteristics: quantity of work and personal characteristics. In four of five districts wide differences are apparent for quantity of work. In two districts differences of over 25 percent are apparent for personal characteristics. At the departmental level the largest difference pertains to quantity of work indicators. We believe that supervisors were not willing to mention quantity of work as an indicator they stress because it would

TABLE 3.2 Patrol Officer and Supervisor Perceptions of Performance Indicators by District

Each cell shows Frequency (top) and Col. % (bottom). For each district the left sub-column = Mentions by Officer, right sub-column = Mentions by Supervisor.

Mentions by Officer / Supervisor: Frequency Col. %	A (Officer)	A (Supervisor)	B (Officer)	B (Supervisor)	C (Officer)	C (Supervisor)	D (Officer)	D (Supervisor)	E (Officer)	E (Supervisor)	Row Total (Officer)	Row Total (Supervisor)
Quantity of work	25 / 80.6	2 / 33.3	6 / 25.0	1 / 20.0	21 / 70.0	1 / 33.3	22 / 62.9	0 / 0.	18 / 62.1	1 / 20.0	92 / 61.7	5 / 20.8
Work characteristics/habits	17 / 54.8	3 / 50.0	10 / 41.7	3 / 60.0	14 / 46.7	1 / 33.3	13 / 37...	2 / 40.0	21 / 44.8	2 / 40.0	75 / 50.3	11 / 45.8
Quality of work	12 / 38.7	2 / 33.3	12 / 50.0	2 / 40.0	11 / 36.7	1 / 33.3	15 / 42.9	3 / 60.0	13 / 44.8	1 / 20.0	63 / 42.3	9 / 37.5
Quality of paperwork	10 / 32.3	3 / 50.0	2 / 8.3	0 / 0.	3 / 10.0	0 / 0.	5 / 14.3	0 / 0.	6 / 20.7	0 / 0.	26 / 17.4	3 / 12.5
Personal characteristics	12 / 38.7	3 / 50.0	13 / 54.2	1 / 20.0	8 / 26.7	1 / 33.3	15 / 42.9	4 / 80.0	13 / 44.8	2 / 40.0	61 / 40.9	11 / 45.8
Desire to do work	8 / 25.8	1 / 16.7	12 / 50.0	2 / 40.0	9 / 30.0	1 / 33.3	14 / 40.0	2 / 40.0	10 / 34.5	1 / 20.0	53 / 35.6	7 / 29.2
Civil service criteria	NA / NA	1 / 16.7	NA / NA	0 / 0.	NA / NA	0 / 0.	NA / NA	0 / 0.	NA / NA	0 / 0.	NA / NA	1 / 4.2
Total number of respondents	31 / 20.8	6 / 25.0	24 / 16.1	5 / 20.8	30 / 20.1	3 / 12.5	35 / 23.5	5 / 20.8	29 / 19.5	5 / 20.8	N=149 / 100.0	N=24 / 100.0

cast a poor reflection on the orientation they take toward patrol officers' work.

In order to assess how supervisors influence officer perceptions of their work, we cross-tabulated officers' self-rating of their work by indicators that direct supervisors emphasize. Officers were asked to rate the quality of their work performance on a scale that included codes of outstanding, good, average, below average, and poor. No officer rated his or her performance as below average or poor. Those who rated themselves as outstanding, 16.2 percent, have a tendency to mention quality of work, quality of paperwork, personal or psychological characteristics, and desire to do work more frequently than those who rated themselves as good or average (Table 3.3). From this table, one can infer that when officers have a high rating of their performance it may in part be due to the emphasis placed on quality and proactivity. In contrast, officers who rate their work of lesser qualities believe that their supervisors emphasize quantity indicators. It was also found that in a comparison of quality of work to other indicators, officers who said their supervisors stress quality were slightly more likely to state that their supervisors' judgments were more important to them (tabular results not shown).

Quantity of work measures had been determined to be the most frequently mentioned (by officers) performance indicator emphasized by supervisors. One might logically expect that when supervisors emphasize quantity and when officers try to meet supervisory expectations, the highest amount of activity will come from these officers. It has also been determined that supervisors' emphasis on quantity has a slight, negative association with officer self-rating. In essence, the preceding two statements suggest divergent hypotheses. The first is drawn from the assumptions of the command model that supervisor use of hierarchical authority directs work activity leading to desired outputs (arrests). The latter, based on empirical findings, reinforces the bargaining model assertion that officers are independent of supervision and those who feel efficacious about doing work (making arrests) are not as subject to supervisory direction.

The interest now is in determining whether an emphasis on quantity of work is in fact related to actual arrest rates. To do this, we examined officers who have been assigned to the district for at least a year and who work in the ten districts for which we have complete supervisor data (both sergeant and lieutenant). We created a variable that has two categories: neither platoon supervisor explicitly mentioned an emphasis on quantity, and one of the platoon's supervisors mentioned an emphasis on quantity

TABLE 3.3   Supervisor's Emphasized Indicators by Officer Self-Rating of Importance

Frequency col. %	Self-Rating of Performance			
	Outstanding	Good	Average	Row Total
Quality of work	11	55	25	91
	45.8	63.2	67.6	61.5
Work characteristics/ habits	6	47	21	74
	25.0	54.0	56.8	50
Quality of work	11	39	12	62
	45.8	44.8	32.4	41.9
Quality of paperwork	5	17	4	26
	20.8	19.5	10.8	17.6
Personal or psychological characteristics	12	35	14	61
	50.0	40.2	37.8	41.2
Desire to do work	10	33	10	53
	41.7	37.9	27.0	35.8
Column total	24	87	37	N=148
	16.2	58.8	25.0	

(Table 3.4). The pattern of effects in Table 3.4 suggests a weak relationship (not statistically significant at .05) between whether quantity was mentioned by supervisors and officer arrest rates. Officer arrest behavior does not appear to be influenced by supervisor emphasis on quantity of work.

An analysis similar to that shown in Table 3.4 was also conducted, but this time the officer's belief that the supervisor emphasized quantity of work was examined, not the platoon supervisor's comment. Although these results are not shown, it was determined that a very slight (not statistically significant at the .05 level) relationship is evident between officers' arrest output and officers' belief that their direct supervisors emphasize quantity of work. In other words, those officers who said their supervisors emphasized quantity of work did not produce more arrests.

Not all districts in the department have the same service conditions. Certainly some districts have more crime than others. In the higher crime

TABLE 3.4   Arrests by Supervisor Emphasis on Quantity of Work

Arrests	Frequency Col.%	Quantity Not Mentioned by Supervisor	Quantity Mentioned by Supervisor	Row Total
1st quartile		12 28.6	11 21.6	23 24.7
2nd quartile		11 26.2	11 26.2	22 23.7
3rd quartile		8 19.0	15 29.4	23 24.7
4th quartile		11 26.2	14 27.5	25 26.9
Gamma = .13 not sig. at .05	Column Total	42 45.2	51 54.8	N = 93*

*N represents 10 districts and no officers with less than one year service in the district. district.

areas, more potential exists for officers to make arrests than in the low crime areas. In order to develop some kind of control for differential demand, we computed an average arrest rate for each district. The assumption is that arrests within the district should be uniform because platoons rotate shifts every 28 days (this does not apply to one district in which shift assignments are constant). We found that officers' belief that direct supervisors emphasize quantity of work had a moderate influence on district arrest output in 2 of the 10 platoons, a weak influence on 1 platoon and no influence in 3 others. In 4 platoons the pattern of results exhibited a slight, negative relationship between officer belief that quantity is emphasized and arrest output. The pattern of effects at the district level is also mixed. Further statistical elaboration is not possible, given the low number of platoon- and district-level respondents.

Another way to examine the question of whether supervisor emphasis on quantity has a bearing on actual officer output is to look at quotas for work. Roughly one-third of the officers who have been with a district for more than one year indicated that their direct supervisors have either stated a number or verbally created an expectation that sets activity quotas. It appears that quotas have a weak, negative effect on officer arrest

TABLE 3.5   Arrests by Officer Belief the Supervisors Have Quotas for Work*

Frequency Col.%	Quotas Not Mentioned	Quotas Mentioned	Row Total
1st quartile	21	17	38
	23.3	37.0	27.9
2nd quartile	21	10	31
	23.3	21.7	22.8
3rd quartile	22	9	31
	24.4	19.6	22.8
4th quartile	26	10	36
	28.9	21.7	26.5
Gamma = –.21 Column	90	46	N = 136**
not sig. at .05 Total	66.2	33.8	

*citations, arrests and warrants
**N represents those in the district for more than one year

output (Table 3.5). In other words, officers who say quotas are mentioned by supervisors are not likely to generate higher levels of arrest output. These findings concerning quotas make sense, given the likelihood that supervisors would try to impose some expectation of work output on those officers who are low producers. Those officers who are high producers obviously need less prodding to produce. One can infer that either supervisors' hierarchical authority is not sufficiently strong to induce performance or supervisory hierarchical control is not an appropriate way to induce performance. The latter thought is consistent with the bargaining model notion that officers have few problems evading supervisory demands.

CONCLUSIONS AND POLICY IMPLICATIONS

In this chapter we have argued that individual officer performance is a multifaceted concept. Supervisors place considerable emphasis on easily quantifiable measures such as arrests. When quantity measures are emphasized by supervisors, patrol officers are likely to believe that such measures are not appropriate performance indicators. Conversely, when quality of work measures are emphasized by supervisors, officers are likely to believe that such measures are appropriate performance indicators.

The influence of first-line supervisors in directing the behavior of officers is seriously limited. Even though supervisors emphasize a particular performance criterion or suggest that a certain level of performance be met, officers under their command do not seem to respond positively to these cues.

Our previous research on police supervision has led us to challenge prevalent police textbook wisdom (Garner, 1981; Iannoe, 1970; Melnicoe and Menning, 1978; Trojanowicz, 1980) concerning supervisory control and to embrace the developing observation-based police literature, which suggests limited supervisory control. Time and time again after we conducted the formal interview and settled down in the car to observe the supervisor in the street setting, we were asked if we really understood what supervision was like. We eventually explained some of our earlier findings, such as those that address the limited effect supervision has on officers' actions and getting officers to do work (Allen, 1979, 1982), but the supervisors (who do not deal with empirical patterns and trends) usually had a more cut-and-dried notion about their work. They frequently stated that in the final analysis, some officers can be directed or controlled and some cannot. With that assertion behind them, the supervisors often go on to tell stories of how they managed finally to determine what motivates a formerly indolent officer and how that individual's attitude and performance turned around. In the next breath, they tell the story of the officer who does virtually nothing right, and the best the supervisor can do, because he cannot fire the officer, is assign the person to a beat where he does the least harm.

Comments of this nature concerning street supervision as well as the developing body of knowledge about the effect of supervision on officer behavior lead us to believe that police managers and policymakers throughout the country who may be skeptical of our findings will eventually have to come to terms with a fundamental question: Given the serious constraints on supervisors to direct officer behavior, what adaptions can be made to increase officers' motivational inducements to improve their performance? Currently, many supervisors who provide inducements overlook departmental operating procedures to create positive bargaining positions for themselves, certainly an undesirable condition for those who should promote compliance to rules.

An appropriate policy idea is the restructuring of performance inducements in order to emphasize positive incentives and deemphasize the preponderance of negative incentives. Currently, some of this restructuring is being accomplished by career development strategies, such as the master-patrolman rank and differential pay increases. Imprecise measurement, fiscal retrenchment, and police unions present formidable obstacles to implementing such policies, however.

A more general policy orientation concerns the idea of "experimental management" (Landau and Stout, 1979: 152). They stress that

> it bears much repetition, then, that solutions to problems cannot be commanded. They must be discovered: found on the basis of imagination, analysis, experiment and criticism.

Police managers must be willing to recognize the limitations of rigid control procedures and to experiment with more flexible response. The introduction of flexibility to create inducements squares with our bargaining model notion that different officers respond to different incentives. Supervisors, as mid-level managers, occupy the right position to translate departmental objectives into operational policy. If supervisors are allowed a freer hand to experiment and innovate, they will be able to determine the appropriate set of inducements to bargain for desired work output.

NOTES

1. During the years 1965 to 1973, six national commissions were convened to address the issues concerning the police role in modern society. Perhaps the most frequently cited are the American Bar Association (1973) and the President's Commission (1967).

2. This chapter examines the topic of individual patrol officer performance, not agency performance. Of course, the two performance concepts are related; agency-level performance is in a large part an aggregate of individual-level performance. Some agency level performance issues, however, are not pertinent at the individual level, such as citizen perceptions of fear and behavioral adaptations due to fear. Individual officer actions certainly have an influence on citizen fear of crime, but it is not possible to disaggregate a community-level sense of fear and attribute portions of it to individual officers.

3. Like any other quantitative evidence, results engendered from multiple indicators involve judgments in interpretation. Some of the difficulties of determining the validity of a single measure are less a problem with multiple indicators. With multiple

indicators the interpretation of results is based on a consistent pattern (and perhaps magnitude) of effects. Often the interpretation of a pattern of effects is not straightforward, but such a judgment may be more reliable than an interpretation based on one indicator.

4. Problems also exist with internal control over the collection of data. Whitaker et al. (1980) note that little attention within an agency is given to the process of data collection.

5. Also see Tifft (1975) for a discussion of supervisory reward power.

6. In our coding we did not double code any value; that is, we did not use the same value more than one time per case. For example, if "arrests" was the first mention and "citations" was the second mention, only one code was assigned: quantity of work.

7. The variable denoting officer perception of indicators that supervisors emphasize was created by using the SPSS Multi-Response subroutine. Cell frequencies total to more than row or column totals due to the multiple mentions. Row, column, and total N represent number of respective respondents.

REFERENCES

ALLEN, D. N. (1979) "The effect of street-level supervision on police officer actions," presented at the annual meeting of the Midwest Political Science Association, Chicago.

——— (1982) "Police supervision on the street: an analysis of supervisor/officer interaction during the shift." Journal of Criminal Justice 10: 91-109.

American Bar Association (1973) The Urban Police Function. Chicago: American Bar Association.

BITTNER, E. (1970) The Functions of Police in Modern Society. Washington, DC: U.S. Government Printing Office.

BROWN, M. K. (1981) Working the Street. New York: Russell Sage.

DOWNS, A. (1967) Inside Bureaucracy. Boston: Little, Brown.

FARR, J. L. and F. J. LANDY (1979) "The development and use of supervisory and peer scales for police performance appraisal," in C. Spielberger (ed.) Police Selection and Evaluation. New York: Praeger.

GARNER, G. W. (1981) Police Supervision. Springfield, IL: Charles C. Thomas.

HEPBURN, J. R. (1981) "Crime Control, Due Process, and the Measurement of Police Performance." Journal of Police Science and Administration 9: 88-98.

IANNOE, N. F. (1970) Supervision of Police Personnel. Englewood Cliffs, NJ: Prentice-Hall.

JACOBS, R. (1981) "Discrepancies in performance evaluations of police officers." Police Chief (January): 30, 31, 62.

JONES, J. M. (1980) Organizational Aspects of Police Behavior. Farnborough, England: Gower.

KOHLAN, R. G. (1973) "Police promotional procedures in fifteen jurisdictions." Public Personnel Management 2: 167-170.

LaFAVE, W. (1965) Arrest: The Decision to Take a Suspect into Custody. Boston: Little, Brown.

LANDAU, M. and R. STOUT (1979) "To manage is not to control: or the folly of Type II errors." Public Administration Review 39: 148-156.

LEFKOWITZ, J. (1975) "Psychological attitudes of policement – a review of research and opinion." Journal of Social Issues 31: 3-26.

MARX, G. T. (1978) "Alternative measures of police performance," in R. Larson (ed.) Police Accountability. Lexington, MA: D. C. Heath.

MAXFIELD, M. G., D. N. ALLEN, and G. E. ANTUNES (1981) "The role of street-level supervisors in police patrol operations," presented at the annual meeting of the American Society of Criminology, Washington, D.C.

MELNICOE, W. B. and J. C. MENNING (1978) Elements of Police Supervision. Encino, CA: Glencoe.

NADEL, S. W. (1979) "Measurement systems and organizational goals in a large metropolitan police department." Police Studies 1: 39-45.

OSTROM, E. (1973) "On the meaning and measurement of output and efficiency in the provision of urban police services." Journal of Criminal Justice 1: 93-112.

PARKS, R. B. (1975) "Sources and limitations of data in criminal justice research," in J. A. Gardiner and M. A. Mulkey (eds.) Crime and Criminal Justice. Lexington, MA: D. C. Heath.

PERRY, D. and P. A. SORNOFF (1973) Politics at the Street-Level: The Select Case of Police Administration and the Community. Beverly Hills, CA: Sage.

President's Commission on Law Enforcement and Administration of Justice (1967) Task Force Report: The Police. Washington, DC: U.S. Government Printing Office.

PROTTAS, J. M. (1978) "The power of the street-level bureaucrat in public service bureaucracies." Urban Affairs Quarterly 13: 285-312.

RICCO, L. J. and J. F. HEAPHY (1977) "Apprehension productivity of police in large U.S. cities." Journal of Criminal Justice 5: 271-278.

REPETTO, T. A. (1980) "Police organization and management," in R. Starfengerger (ed.) Progress in Policing: Essays on Change. Cambridge, MA: Ballinger.

RHEAD, C., A. ABRAMS, H. TROSMAN, and P. MARGOLIS (1968) "The psychological assessment of police candidates." American Journal of Psychiatry 124: 575-584.

RUBINSTEIN, J. (1973) City Police. New York: Ballantine.

SHARP, E. (1982) "Police performance measurement: reactions and a further suggestion. Urban Interest 4: 34-40.

SHERMAN, L. W. and B. GLICK (1980) The Validity of Arrest Rates for Cross-Sectional Analysis. Washington, DC: Police Foundation.

SKOGAN, W. G. (1976) "Citizen reporting of crime: some national panel data." Criminology 13: 530-542.

――― and G. E. ANTUNES (1979) "Information, apprehension, and deterrence: exploring the limits of police productivity." Journal of Criminal Justice 7: 217-256.

SKOLNICK, J. H. (1966) Justice Without Trial. New York: John Wiley.

STEVENS, J. M. and J. C. McDAVID (1981)."Urban police performance attitudes." Computers, Environment and Urban Systems 6: 157-169.

TIFFT, L. L. (1975) "Control systems, social bases of power and power exercise in police organizations." Journal of Police Science and Administration 3: 66-76.

TROJANOWICZ, R. C. (1980) The Environment of the First-Line Supervisor. Englewood Cliffs, NJ: Prentice-Hall.

VAN MANNEN, J. (1974) "Working the street: a developmental view of police behavior," in H. Jacob (ed.) The Potential for Reform in Criminal Justice. Beverly Hills, CA: Sage.

WHITAKER, G., S. MASTROFSKI, E. OSTROM, R. P. PARKS, and S. L. PERCY (1980) Measuring Police Agency Performance. Washington, DC: National Institute of Justice.

WICE, P. B. (1978) Criminal Lawyers. Beverly Hills, CA: Sage.

II.

Stress and Attrition

Central to the notion of a police working environment is consideration of the environment's most basic element: police personnel. Whereas personnel research and policy analysis in the 1970s focused almost exclusively on personnel selection, testing, education, and training, policy research in the 1980s investigates the impact of the police occupation on the individual officer and his or her reaction to it.

Primary among the important occupational impacts are job stress and dissatisfaction, which not only detract from the officer's ability to perform police tasks effectively but also lead to attrition from the ranks. As police departments face severe budget constraints, the implications of reduced effectiveness of personnel, and the loss of recruitment, selection and training investments through attrition become more profound and damaging to the police delivery of crime-related services.

The two chapters in Part II critically investigate the sources and effects of job-related stress and dissatisfaction in the police working environment. Russo, Engel, and Hatting have investigated the important question of the sources and symptoms of police stress. They convincingly argue that the sources and symptoms vary based on three empirically derived types of police officers and three definitions (organizational, situational, and other) of the working environment. The authors relate the sources of stress to types of officers and working environments and uncover a wide spectrum of interesting and pervasive symptoms of stress. The policy implications of their findings—that generalized, quick-fix directives will not lessen stress and its costly consequences—cannot be overlooked. Effective departmental policy must recognize the complexity of the stress issue, and action programs directed toward it must be multifaceted.

Chapter 5, by Sparger and Giacopassi, continues the investigation of stress and dissatisfaction within the police working environment. Rather than focusing exclusively on stress, the authors attempt to explain how stress and dissatisfaction lead to untimely and voluntary attrition. They argue that the current explanatory models of stress and dissatisfaction are inadequate. They propose a new model that incorporates consideration of "turning points," or periods within a career when awareness of a need for change stimulates career movement. The authors empirically found that this combined model best accounted for the occurrence of voluntary resignations. Their findings also cast doubt on current thinking about sources of police attrition. The traditional concerns of salary and family pressures were not related to dissatisfaction or the propensity to leave the force. In contrast, feelings of job stagnation were highly associated with attrition.

These two chapters suggest that the working environment must be modified to enable officers better to cope with stress and job dissatisfaction. Both problems require multifaceted action programs to deal with the symptoms and the underlying feelings, and to counteract a sense of job stagnation. The quality of the working environment and the delivery of police services in the 1980s depend on these policy issues being addressed.

4.

POLICE AND OCCUPATIONAL STRESS:
An Empirical Investigation

Philip A. Russo, Jr.
Alan S. Engel
Miami University

Steven H. Hatting
College of St. Thomas

Occupational stress stands out as a dominant theme in police research. Studies such as "Burned-Out Cops and Their Families" by Christina Maslach and Susan Jackson (1979) and Robert J. McGuire's "The Human Dimension of Urban Policing: Dealing with Stress in the 1980s" (1979) are illustrative of the interest in this topic that has emerged in the literature. Such research ranges from Maslach and Jackson's efforts to "measure" the "levels of stress" in a group of individual officers and their families, to McGuire's theoretical formulations concerning the sources of tension and the indicators of stress.

In fact, the topic is not altogether new. It would be more accurate to say that current research has taken up the useful lead first presented some two decades earlier in the form of Hans Selye's (1956) *The Stress of Life.* In his seminal work, Selye gauges both the physical and psychological impact of environmental stress on human subjects. But it was not until the late 1960s that attention refocused on the problems of police stress. Two areas of investigation and writing will explain the linkage to Selye and to the research reported here: first, the literature on police discretion, and second, the identification of police types.

Perhaps the most insightful explanation of the roots of what today is recognized as occupational stress in American law enforcement is Herbert

Packer's (1968) *The Limits of the Criminal Sanction.* The author identifies two competing sets of values in criminal case disposition: crime control and due process. Clashes between them in many phases of police work (on the beat, in the squad car, in the interrogation room) give rise to police discretion.[1]

This elucidation of the bedrock of police discretion greatly accelerated research on the subject. A good example is Peter Manning's (1977) *Police Work.* Manning argues that discretion is an inescapable part of an "impossible mandate" the police are forced to bear in our constitutional system. Fulfillment of this "mandate" will necessarily remain "impossible," Manning contends, because of a dilemma imposed on the police by the judicial interpretation of the Bill of Rights. As Jerome Skolnick (1975) put it in *Justice Without Trial,* law enforcement officers are required to observe the "legal ethic" (due process) while pursuing a "work ethic" (crime control). Police administrators and the public tend to expect both, often failing to realize that procedural fairness and efficiency are incompatible values.[2]

The anxiety produced by these conflicting demands may trigger in part the occupational stress we are investigating here. That such stress, whatever its source, has debilitating effects is well documented by Arthur Niederhoffer and James Ahern. Niederhoffer's (1969) *Behind the Shield* is the successful effort of a veteran police officer to supplement personal experience with survey data. He discovers, for example, widespread cynicism, especially among young patrol officers.[3] Is the cynicism Niederhoffer describes associated with occupational stress? It may be in at least two ways. First, cynicism could be a product of the tension inherent in the job. Second, it could be a primary means officers use to cope with those tensions.

Ahern, a former chief-of-police in New Haven, Connecticut, wrote *Police in Trouble* (1972). He relates from firsthand experience the frustration and disgust officers feel in dealing with a public rarely capable of empathizing with the police. Occupational stress would seem to be a predictable result. The sources and consequences of such stress need to be monitored, then, in order to suggest ways to minimize it.

Another example is Blackmore's (1978) "Are Police Allowed to Have Problems of Their Own?" Blackmore expressed great concern that, in police work more than in other occupations, there is a tendency for stress-related problems to be hidden by officers and ignored by departmental supervisors. The author distinguished four types of stress: (1) external stress related to negative public attitudes, (2) organizational stress due to low pay or similar grievances, (3) performance-related stress stemming from fear, boredom, or schedule, and (4) personal stress such as marital difficulties.

Ellison and Genz's (1978) "Police Officer as Burned-Out Samaritan" presents a clear difference between two kinds of stress in police work: (1) the temporary but acute type resulting from a given encounter, episode, or situation (perhaps a case of child abuse or the death of a fellow officer in the line of duty) and (2) the long-term, chronic sort that arises from departmental assignments (homicide squad) and/or organizational structure (the military model, which downplays the use of independent judgment).

Finally, Martin Reiser's (1976) "Some Organizational Stresses on Policemen" focuses on organizational sources alone. Reiser found internal investigations and individual failure to be promoted to be especially stressful to young officers. He also discusses what is termed the "John Wayne syndrome" within police departments—an authoritarian attitude that spills over into the officer's family relationships. This outlook, coupled with the so-called 'jackass fallacy'—a conviction among higher-ranking officers that motivation among the rank-and-file depends on the proverbial carrot-and-stick approach—undermines morale, destroys marriages, and generally produces constant anxiety both on duty and off.

Second, a brief examination of the literature on police types should remind us of the limits of generalizing about police behavior among departments or even within any one of them. We should not assume that a particular department or individual officer performs in a prescribed way. James Q. Wilson's (1968) *Varieties of Police Behavior* is especially noteworthy in a theoretical sense. He distinguishes three "styles" of policing from a departmental perspective: what he calls the "watchman," the "legalistic," and the "service" orientations. Wilson's framework can be linked directly to William Ker Muir's (1977) *Police: Streetcorner Politicians*. What Wilson accomplished at the departmental level, Muir does with individual officers. Muir himself notes the congruence between his "avoider" and Wilson's "watchman" posture, his "reciprocator" and Wilson's "service" ambience, his "enforcer" and Wilson's "legalistic" style.

Muir (1977: 296) concludes with a lament: The police literature is virtually "bereft of sophisticated portaits of any individual patrolmen who grew in office. . . . The literature does not tell us how a policeman can develop a morality enabling him to be mean opportunistically without becoming mean compulsively." Could the reason for this absence of what Muir describes as "professionalism" among individual officers lie in the realm of occupational stress? To what extent might different styles of or attitudes toward the police function relate to an officer's susceptibility to stress or to his or her method of responding to it? Is the police officer's working environment (not only value conflict but also personal danger and human tragedy) so overwhelming in varied forms of stress that "previously felt obligations to be reasonable, kind, emphathetic, and creative" (Muir, 1977: 296) are eclipsed? Wilson's and Muir's perceptive studies led us to ask these and related questions.

METHOD

Data were obtained from four medium-sized, midwestern police departments. Medium-sized departments were operationalized as those with from 40 to 125 full-time, uniformed officers. A pretested survey instrument was administered to 225 police officers generating 173 valid responses. Respondents represented all ranks of officers in the police departments of Fairfield, Hamilton, and Middletown, Ohio, and Richmond, Indiana. Out of the 77 percent response rate, 35 percent were from Hamilton, 25 percent were from Middletown, 23 percent were from Richmond, and 17 percent were from Fairfield. Table 4.1 provides a demographic profile of the 173 respondents. It indicates that the typical police officer in this study was modestly educated, with 10 or fewer years experience, between the ages of 21 and 35, male, and a product of a working-class home.

The survey instrument was a comprehensive questionnaire including both open-ended and forced-choice questions, designed to obtain demographic information, attitudes of police officers toward their job, symptoms of stress, and sources of stress. The questionnaire incorporated elements of survey items utilized in previously published police research. Specifically, indicators used to obtain and organize data on the sources of police stress were adapted from McGuire (1979). In order to develop measures of occupational/career orientations, the survey instrument drew on attitudinal questions utilized in Rosenberg (1957). To preserve the anonymity of respondents and the integrity of their answers, the instrument was delivered to the individual police officers' mail boxes at department headquarters. The completed questionnaires were then retrieved at a central depository.

As discussed in the previous section, occupational stress has become a major focus in police research. The literature has documented that police work is a particularly stressful occupation with symptoms of stress ranging from such classic physical conditions as ulcers to more complex psychological conditions such as feelings of loss of self-esteem. Table 4.2 provides data on the incidence of symptoms of stress among the police officers in

TABLE 4.1   Demographics (N=173)

44%	10 years and under as police officers
55%	high school education
58%	under age 35
71%	patrolmen
98%	male
62%	fathers were blue-collar workers
39%	fathers had less than high school education
38%	fathers had high school education
60%	mothers were housewives
51%	mothers had high school education

TABLE 4.2   Percentage of Officers Suffering from Various Symptoms (N=173)

Moodiness	44
Nervous anxiety	33
Divorce	24
Loss of self-esteem	17
Arguments at home	16
Ulcers	14
Alcoholism	5
Heart trouble	2

this study. Clearly, the data generally reaffirm what the literature on police stress has concluded. One particular exception is the low incidence (5 percent) of alcoholism reported by respondents. This is a notable deviation from other studies, which have reported the incidence of alcoholism among police officers to be much greater. For example, a 1978 study of 2,300 officers reported serious alcohol problems among 23 percent of the police officers studied (Blackmore, 1978).

Our interest in police stress went beyond the symptoms to include possible sources of stress among these officers. As discussed, prior research has developed various typologies of sources of stress among police officers. We identified three categories of sources of stress: personal-related, other-related, and organization-related.[4] Personal-related sources describe a variety of situations with which the officer may be called on to deal and which have the capacity to place the officer at high risk of injury, such as responding to and confronting an armed robbery in progress. Other-related stress factors describe circumstances in which the officer is less likely to risk personal danger but in which the victimization of someone else may evoke strong feelings of empathy and tension, such as assisting the elderly victim of a mugging. In the third category, organizational stress factors, references are made to the frustrations and problems associated within their own or other agencies in the criminal justice system, such as insensitive supervisors or unsympathetic judicial personnel. Tables 4.3, 4.4, and 4.5 detail those findings.

That domestic violence, weapons calls, and fights in public places rank high as personally stressful situations is not surprising (Table 4.3). Indeed, these data dovetail with the established police view that the situations are unpredictable, high-risk, and have a high potential for injury or something more serious (Skolnick, 1975). However, that traffic stops, responses to silent alarms, and breakings and enterings in progress are ranked by our respondents as much less stressful does not wholly conform with what might have been expected. This anomaly might be explained in two ways: First, it is entirely possible that such incidents in which offenders are still present are infrequent occurrences and, therefore, much less personally threatening; or second, it may well be that our respondents defined the questionnaire item to include only the more common after-the-fact situation that requires only report taking, rather than incidents in which the offenders are still present at the scene.

The data in Table 4.4 do not present any particular deviations from our general understanding of what causes stress among police officers in other-related situations. The high rankings of child abuse, homicide, and rape, compared with the lower rankings of burglary, assault, and in-home injury investigations, correspond to the general patterns of police reactions.

Similarly, Table 4.5 confirms the expected. Police antipathy toward judges and prosecutors is well documented and, as with other workers within organizations, complaints about insensitive supervisors, conflicting job demands, and lack of recognition are quite common (Kroes, 1974).

Although interesting, these data treat our respondents as an aggregate. However, police officers are not an undifferentiated group, and to generalize about all officers in this way is to ignore a distinction of some importance. Distinguishing between different types of police officers aids our understanding and provides insight into the possible variations in their symptoms and sources of stress. Although typologies of police such as Wilson's and Muir's have moved us beyond the more conventional view of police as all of one stripe, the central focus has been on describing the behavioral styles of policing from a departmental or individual perspective.

TABLE 4.3   Personal-Related Sources of Stress (N=173)

Stress Factor	*Median*
3 most important	
Domestic violence	1.8
Weapons calls	2.2
Fights in public places	3.2
3 least important	
Traffic stops	6.2
Silent alarms	5.6
B&E in progress	4.1

NOTE: 1 = most stressful; 7 = least stressful.

TABLE 4.4   Other-Related Sources of Stress (N=173)

Stress Factor	*Median*
3 most important	
Child abuse	1.0
Homicide	2.9
Rape	3.2
3 least important	
Burglary investigations	7.5
Assault investigations	6.6
In-home injury	5.7

NOTE: 1 = most stressful; 8 = least stressful.

TABLE 4.5   Organizational-Related Sources of Stress (N=173)

Stress Factor	*Median*
Unresponsive judges	1.3
Uncooperative prosecutors	2.3
Insensitive supervisors	3.3
Conflicting job demands	3.5
Lack of recognition	3.6

NOTE: 1 = most stressful; 5 = least stressful.

However, the sources and symptoms of occupational stress have not been the primary focus of these typologies.

We hypothesized that an understanding of different occupational/career motivations of police officers and being able to differentiate conceptually among these motivations are critical to the explanation of various problems of police stress.

Individuals who choose police work, like those who choose a career in sales promotion, carpentry, or teaching, do so for a wide variety of reasons. Obviously a number of factors influence career decisions: socioeconomic status, education, family and peer pressures, chance opportunities, and so on. However, what we are concerned with in this study are the value orientations of career choice.

When an individual chooses law enforcement as a career, certain values inform that occupational decision. Opting to become a police officer is not a value in and of itself, but the decision is made on the basis of certain previously formed values. In essence, these values reflect a motivational dimension regarding what an individual wants out of his or her work and, to some extent, what he or she wants out of life.[5]

To obtain information about what values were important in choosing a career as a police officer, we asked respondents to rank 12 items as to the degree of importance they played in their decision to become a police officer. Table 4.6 provides a list of these items.

These 12 items may be grouped according to three primary underlying values that inform an individual officer's choice of police work as an occupation. Items 1 through 4 might be called "people-oriented values." Officers who rank these items as important would tend to view police work as an opportunity to derive satisfaction from working with people. "Professional-self-oriented values" are identified in items 5 through 8. Officers who rank these factors as important would tend to view police work as an opportunity for achieving their self-perceived potential and utilizing their self-perceived talents. Finally, items 9 through 12 might be called "personal-reward-oriented values." Officers who rank these items as important would tend to view police work as a means to a personal reward. Personal rewards are desired *for* police work rather than *from* police work.[6]

Factor analyses were performed to identify the underlying commonalities of the respondents' rankings of importance of the 12 items. This technique resulted in the clustering of the respondents' rankings into three distinct groups. The first cluster includes those officers who had ranked personal-reward values as most important to their decision to become a

TABLE 4.6   Career Choice Values (N=173)

(1)	Chance to be of service to people.
(2)	Chance to work with people, not things.
(3)	Chance to look out for public interest.
(4)	Chance to use professional skills in a creative manner.
(5)	Chance to think and act independently on the job.
(6)	Chance to work with highly qualified and motivated people.
(7)	Chance to advance to a position of authority and responsibility.
(8)	High prestige in the public eye.
(9)	Good salary.
(10)	Good working conditions.
(11)	Good fringe benefits.
(12)	Job security.

police officer. The second cluster includes those officers that had ranked people-oriented values as most important to their decision to become a police officer. The third cluster consists of those officers who had ranked professional-career-oriented values as most important in their decision to become a police officer. Table 4.7 identifies the three clusters and the variables that loaded onto those factors.

Factor scores were computed for the three factors generated to obtain a measure of how individual respondents scored on each of the three factors. Respondents were then grouped according to the highest of their three factor scores, provided that their highest factor score was above the median factor score of all respondents. According to this test, we assumed that the respondent possessed the motivational value characterized by his or her highest factor score. This process accounted for approximately 81 percent (140) of all respondents. Table 4.8 identifies the three types.

Having classified approximately 81 percent of our respondents into three types, we can now focus on the possible differences among them with respect to both the symptoms and the sources of stress.

TYPES AND STRESS

Demographic profiles of these three types of police officers reveal some interesting patterns. Those officers holding primarily economic and security values—personal reward orientations—were generally older, more experienced, and higher-ranking officers. For example, almost half (47 percent) had over 10 years' experience as a police officer. Forty-one percent were over the age of 35, and more than one-third (35 percent)

TABLE 4.7   Cluster Analysis of Career Choice Values (N=173)

	Variable	*Factor Loading*
Cluster 1	work conditions	.86
	salary	.84
	fringe benefits	.74
	job security	.45
Cluster 2	service to people	.84
	working with people, not things	.68
	protecting the public	.65
Cluster 3	advance to position of authority	.66
	use professional skills	.60
	independence on job	.54
	high prestige	.46

TABLE 4.8   Distribution of Respondents Among Types

Group 1	*Group 2*	*Group 3*
Personal reward N = 47	People-oriented N = 52	Professional career N = 41

held the rank of sergeant or above. In contrast, those officers who were motivated by people-oriented values were characteristically younger, less experienced, and relatively better educated. For example, nearly two-thirds (65.8 percent) had been police officers for less than 10 years. Moreover, 65 percent were below the age of 35, and over one-half (52 percent) of these officers had graduated from high school, with an overwhelming majority of these having completed two or more years of college. The third type of officers, those who were motivated by professional career values, proved to be the most experienced, with an average length of service as a police officer of approximately 13 years. Moreover, this was the oldest group, with 51 percent age 35 or over. Surprisingly, 70 percent had only a high school education, and 85 percent of these police officers held the rank of patrolman.

With a typology that helps us better to understand who our police officers are and what their occupational orientations are, we can more clearly focus on variations in the symptoms and sources of stress among these types of police.

The data indicate an above-average incidence of ulcers (15 percent) among those officers with a personal reward orientation. Moreover, these officers reported a 9 percent rate of alcoholism, a percentage above that of the undifferentiated pool. Comparatively, officers holding a personal reward orientation evidenced rates for these two stress symptoms well above those reported by the other two groups of officers. Finally, these officers reported a relatively high (34 percent) incidence of nervous anxiety. Where personal-reward-oriented officers had noticeably fewer than average symptoms was in their reported rates of feelings of loss of self-esteem and arguments at home.

The second group of officers, those whose occupational orientation may be characterized as people-oriented, evidenced much different symptoms of stress. These officers reported the highest rates of divorce (30 percent) and arguments at home (25 percent). In addition, this group reported slightly above-average feelings of loss of self-esteem. In contrast, they were identifiably below average with respect to three stress symptoms: alcoholism, ulcers, and moodiness.

Finally, the professionally oriented police officers exhibited high rates of stress symptoms with respect to moodiness (50 percent), nervous anxiety (40 percent), and feelings of loss of self-esteem (24 percent). These reported rates were well above average and greater than either of the other two groups of police officers. This group evidenced comparatively lower rates of reported stress symptoms with respect to home arguments (14 percent), and ulcers (11 percent). Table 4.9 provides a summary of the incidence of stress among the three types.

Data on the sources of stress also reveal some interesting patterns among the three types. With respect to organizational sources of stress, the most common lament among all three groups was over unresponsive judges and uncooperative prosecutors. However, insensitive supervisors were cited most often as problems by those officers with a professional career orientation, and least often by the personal-reward-oriented police officer. Pressures arising from the conflicting job demands of a police officer were ranked highest by people-oriented officers and lowest by the personal-reward-oriented group. Finally, lack of recognition and rewards was ranked as a more serious problem by personal-reward-oriented officers and ranked least serious by the people-oriented group. Table 4.10 summarizes these data.

TABLE 4.9   Police Types and Stress Symptoms

	Personal-Reward-Oriented	People-Oriented	Professionally-Oriented
Ulcers	+	−	−
Nervous anxiety	+	−	+
Alcoholism	+	−	−
Divorce	−	+	−
Moodiness	−	−	+
Arguments at home	−	+	−
Loss of self-esteem	−	+	+

NOTE: + = above average; − = below average.

TABLE 4.10   Organizational Sources of Stress by Police Type

	Personal-Reward Oriented	People-Oriented	Professionally-Oriented
Unresponsive judges	H	H	H
Uncooperative prosecutors	H	H	H
Lack of recognition and rewards	H	L	L
Insensitive supervisors	L	L	H
Conflicting job demands	L	H	L

NOTE: H = high; L = low.

Perhaps the most obvious sources of stress for police officers are situations in which their personal safety may be jeopardized. Accordingly, we sought information on these personal-related sources of stress among our three types. The data indicate that the professionally oriented officers reported higher average rankings of these situations; however, the other two groups of police officers were not without stress from the same source. For all three groups, domestic violence and weapons calls were clearly the most stressful types of situations. However, while personal reward and professionally oriented types identified domestic violence situations as most stressful, the people-oriented officers placed weapons calls at the top of their list. Responding to fights in public places was ranked more stressful by professionally oriented officers and least stressful by personal-reward-oriented officers. This was also the case with respect to breakings and enterings in progress. Finally, hot pursuit situations were most stressful for personal-reward-oriented officers and least for the people-oriented types. Table 4.11 summarizes these findings.

The data on our third source of stress—other-related situations—also indicate that police officers suffer the effects of stress from officer-victim contact. Child abuse was uniformly ranked highest by all three groups of officers. However, as with other sources of stress, variations among the three groups are discernible. For example, homicide was ranked most stressful by the people-oriented police officers and least stressful by the personal-reward-oriented group. Rape was reported to be a more stressful situation by professionally oriented officers and a less stressful situation by people-oriented officers. This pattern held true for personal injury accidents as well. Table 4.12 provides a summary of these data.

An analysis of these data leads to a number of explanations that may shed light on the relationships between police types and stress. First, with respect to the personal-reward-oriented officers, we find a unique stress profile. We can assume that these officers entered law enforcement with an eye toward bettering their circumstances of employment and that they reflect a work ethic that embraces economic and other tangible rewards. In other words, their occupational orientation views police work essentially as a basic means of earning a wage and achieving employment security, less than a "calling" or a mission in life (see Niederhoffer, 1969). In support of this, that these officers are older, more experienced, and modestly educated dovetails with the finding that "in the past, job security was rated highest in the police applicant's need hierarchy" (Reiser, 1976: 249). If that is indeed the case, then it is reasonable to expect that officers who come to police work primarily in quest of a paycheck will be particularly stressed by a set of responsibilities and circumstances that are unlike those of other wage-earning routines. In other words, we think one plausible explanation revolves around the physically "shocking" factor in the police routine for a group of workers who had very different images of what they would do to earn that paycheck. Police work is not just another fungible job. As studies have shown, prolonged stress from police work can result in such physical problems as tissue damage and increases in both heart rate and systolic blood pressure (Walrod, 1978). That the personal-reward-oriented officers ranked the lack of recognition and rewards as a more

TABLE 4.11 Personal Safety Sources of Stress by Police Type

	Personal-Reward Oriented	*People-Oriented*	*Professionally-Oriented*
Domestic violence	H	H	H
Weapons calls	H	H	H
Fights in public places	L	L	H
Breaking & entering in progress	L	L	H
Hot pursuit	H	L	H
Traffic stops	L	L	L
Silent alarm calls	L	L	L

NOTE: H = high; L = low.

TABLE 4.12 Other-Related Sources of Stress by Police Type

	Personal-Reward Oriented	*People-Oriented*	*Professionally Oriented*
Child abuse	H	H	H
Homicide	L	H	L
Rape	L	L	H
Personal injury accidents	L	L	H
Drownings	H	L	H
In-home injury	L	L	L
Assault investigation	L	L	L
Burglary investigation	L	L	L

NOTE: H = high; L = low.

serious problem than did the other two types of officers is consistent with their occupational orientation. Clearly, this is a unique organizational source of stress for these police officers. That they are in personal danger and dealing with the "criminal element" of society clashes with their conventional working-class expectations. Moreover, it will be recalled that these officers ranked highest both domestic violence and hot pursuit as personal stress situations. Since the high risk of personal danger is great under these circumstances, we may again conclude that these situations fly in the face of a traditional career orientation that is not congruent with these frequent police encounters. Finally, that this group of officers reported comparatively lower rankings on the other-related stress situations points to the saliency of their personal reward orientation.

On the other hand, those officers whom we characterized as people-oriented types also have a distinct stress profile. These younger, less experienced, and above-average educated officers pursued a career in law enforcement to help others, to protect the public—in other words, to fulfill an obligation to the community: "The young officer is typically idealistic, intelligent and eager. One of his primary motivations in entering the police profession is a desire to help in the community" (Reiser, 1976: 249).

It is interesting to note that this group of officers primarily manifested such symptoms of stress as divorce, frequent arguments at home, and some feeling of a loss of self-esteem. This pattern seems to fall into a category of stress intruding into their domestic relations. Divorce and arguments at home are common symptoms plaguing the police officer. As one study reports, the police officer "unwittingly becomes more tough and aggressive when dealing with his family, questions them more often, and appears to mistrust them; he may become more rigid in deciding what's wrong or right, and less capable of getting emotionally involved with his family. . . . It is almost impossible for policemen to avoid bringing work attitudes home when they leave the station, however valiantly they may try" (Maslach and Jackson, 1979: 61).

That these officers exhibited the highest rates of divorce and arguments at home would seem related to their people orientation—an orientation that places much faith in human ideals and stresses a commitment to other people. This explanation seems to be supported by the fact that this group found the conflicting job demands of a police officer more stressful than either of the other two types. Their orientation frequently conflicts with the realities of police work and, as Niederhoffer (1969) observes, moves the officer from idealism to stressed cynicism. Clearly, these people-oriented officers seem to be taking their problems home.

One unanticipated pattern surfaced from the data on this group. Given their people orientation, one might expect that these officers would report the highest rankings concerning the other-related stress situations. However, we found that they had the lowest rankings. In retrospect, perhaps that is not so surprising after all. If the people-oriented officer has a conception of police-public-victim-perpetrator relationships that does not correspond to reality, it may move such officers to a condition of anomie wherein these stresses are displaced elsewhere—namely, to the home. For example, Lewis (1973) found that police stress emanating from the nature of the employment and conceptualization may be a prime force of anomie.

Our final group, the oldest, most experienced, least educated, and lowest-ranked police officers, who reflect a professional career orientation, present a more traditional profile. Although their orientation is characterized as "professional" and they identified such occupational values as high prestige, independence on the job, and a chance to advance to a position of authority, this group became police officers before the relatively recent move toward higher education and before the drive toward professionalism took root. It can be argued that this group opted for a career in law enforcement while police were still defined as "law enforcers." In other words, for this group professionalism refers more appropriately to a career police orientation that views the officer as a respected public servant, an authority figure, a protector of the community. Indeed, we might see some similarity between this group and the "enforcer" and "legalistic" types of Muir and Wilson respectively.

This group was highly stressed. They reported high rates of nervous anxiety, frequent episodes of moodiness, and substantial feelings of loss of self-esteem since becoming a police officer. Their reported average rankings were highest for personal, other, and organizational sources of stress. For example, they had the highest rankings of unresponsive judges, uncooperative prosecutors, and insensitive supervisors as sources of stress.

The data on these officers provide us with an interesting profile, not without the cynicism to which Niederhoffer refers. They are veteran police officers, modestly educated, limited in career advancement, officers whose unique view of police work did not adjust to the changing realities of law enforcement as an occupation. They may be the nonachievers who have soured on the system. For example, although they, like the personal reward officers, have extended experience as police officers, they do not report the upper-rank positions achieved by the latter. Police work for them may have become a nonrewarding experience. They may have encountered frustration and tension along the way. Their reported moodiness, feelings of loss of self-esteem, and nervous anxiety are understandable within this context. It seems that these officers manifest a unique kind of stress, one that dilutes their enthusiasm and turns them somewhat cynical.

SUMMARY AND CONCLUSIONS

Although this study is preliminary in nature and the conclusions tentative, it does point to some important policy implications for dealing with police stress. First, and primarily, is the understanding that symptoms and sources of stress may vary among different occupationally oriented police types. Although this study classifies police into three types and assesses their respective symptoms and sources of stress, the typology is by no means exhaustive, and further research is invited.

However, an understanding that different occupational orientations may be related to differing problems of stress among police officers may provide guidance for the management and personnel policies within the law enforcement system. Most obviously, in-service training programs and stress reduction practices cannot be applied uniformly. Similarly, recruitment and position assignments need to take account of these differences. Moreover, we would urge a redesign of traditional family support and group therapy programs. Encounter groups with victims and the public in general could likewise profit from an understanding of the differences among police officers. Finally, medical services and psychological counseling programs made available to police officers may become more effective in dealing with police and occupational stress.

NOTES

1. "Discretion" is defined as the authority to make unsupervised, often unreviewable decisions from within a range of sometimes ill-defined choices. Joseph Goldstein (1969) clarifies the choices commonly open to the law enforcement officer. Goldstein's contribution is primarily conceptual—the elaboration of "total," "full," and "actual" levels of enforcement.

2. In a collection of essays, James Q. Wilson (1977) refers to the police as "street-level bureaucrats." He notes appropriately the uniqueness of the criminal justice system with respect to the range of discretionary choice open to its members. Curiously, those at the base of the organizational pyramid, the police, possess a greater measure of discretion, at least in a quantitative sense, than those at the top, the judges.

3. Cynicism is a difficult concept to handle. Perhaps a cynical police officer is one who would answer "none" to the question "What difference does it [anything] make?" or one who takes seriously the perversion of a noble aphorism, "Do unto others before they do unto you."

4. For more detailed discussion, see McGuire (1979).

5. For a more detailed discussion, Rosenberg (1957).

6. Rosenberg, 1957.

REFERENCES

AHERN, J. F. (1972) Police in Trouble. New York: Hawthorn.

BLACKMORE, J. (1978) "Are police allowed to have problems of their own?" Police Magazine 1: 47-55.

BORDUA, D. J. (1967) The Police: Six Sociological Essays. New York: John Wiley.

BRODERICK, J. J. (1979) Police in a Time of Change. Morristown, NJ: General Learning Press.

DAVID, K. (1971) Discretionary Justice. Champaign: University of Illinois Press.

ELLISON, K. W. and J. L. GENZ (1978) "Police officer as burned-out samaritan." FBI Law Enforcement Bulletin 47: 2-7.

GOLDSTEIN, J. (1960) "Police discretion not to invoke the criminal process: low visibility decisions in the administration of justice." Yale Law Journal 69: 543-594.

HAHN, H. (1974) "Profile of urban police," in J. Goldsmith and S. Goldsmith (eds.) Police Community: Dimensions of an Occupational Subculture. Pacific Palisades, CA: Palisades Publishers.

KROES, W. H. (1974) "Psychological stress in police work," presented at the joint colloquium of the Illinois Department of Mental Health and Northwestern University Medical School.

KROES, W. H. and J. J. HURRELL (1975) Job Stress and the Police Officer: Identifying Stress Reduction Techniques. Washington, DC: U.S. Government Printing Office.

LEWIS, R. W. (1973) "Toward an understanding of police anomie." Journal of Police Science and Administration 1: 484-490.

LOTA, R. and R. M. REGOLI (1977) "Police cynicism and professionalism." Human Relations 30: 175-186.

MANNING, P. K. (1977) Police Work. Cambridge, MA: MIT Press.

MASLACH, C. and S. JACKSON (1979) "Burned-out cops and their families." Psychology Today 12: 59-62.

McGUIRE, R. J. (1979) "The human dimension of urban policing: dealing with stress in the 1980s." Police Chief 46: 26-27.

MUIR, W. K. (1977) Police: Streetcorner Politicians. Chicago: University of Chicago Press.

NIEDERHOFFER, A. (1969) Behind the Shield: Police in Urban Society. Garden City, NY: Doubleday.

PACKER, H. (1968) The Limits of the Criminal Sanction. Stanford, CA: Stanford University Press.

REISER, M. (1976) "Some organizational stresses on policemen," in H. W. More, Jr. (ed.) The American Police. St. Paul, MN: West.

REISS, A. (1971) The Police and the Public. New Haven, CT: Yale University Press.

ROSENBERG, M. (1957) Occupations and Values. New York: Free Press.

SELYE, H. (1956) The Stress of Life. New York: McGraw-Hill.

SKOLNICK, J. (1975) Justice Without Trial (2nd ed.). New York: John Wiley.

WALROD, T. H. (1978) "Causes of stress to police officers detailed." National Sheriff 30: 12-29.

WESTLEY, W. (1970) Violence and the Police. Cambridge, MA: MIT Press.

Wickersham Commission (1968) Wickersham Commission Report 14: Report on the Police. Montclair, NJ: Patterson Smith.

WILSON, J. Q. (1968) Varieties of Police Behavior. Cambridge, MA: Harvard Univerversity Press.

———(1977) Thinking About Crime. New York: Random House.

5.

COPPING OUT:
Why Police Leave the Force

Jerry R. Sparger

David J. Giacopassi

Memphis State University

Voluntary attrition or turnover among commissioned police personnel is an issue that has received little attention from the academic community, law enforcement administrators, politicians, or the news media, if articles or speeches on the subject are any index of concern. One more often hears that a local politician or police chief is concerned that funds are unavailable to bring a police department up to authorized strength in order to address more effectively whatever is seen as the paramount problem of that department. To our knowledge, little or no information is presented concerning why the department is under strength, whether the reason is retirement, forced resignation, firing, or voluntary turnover among commissioned personnel. Further, so far as we are able to determine, there is no information available about either the extent of voluntary attrition among police agencies or the causes of this attrition gained from any systematic, empirical study of the subject.

Turnover in a police agency can create problems that are immediately detrimental and time-consuming to resolve. When officers resign, the department must remain short-handed until the process of recruitment, selection, and training can be completed, a process that is not only time-consuming but expensive and that currently must take place in an atmosphere of fiscal austerity or retrenchment. The National Advisory Commission on Criminal Justice Standards and Goals reported in 1973 that the cost for training a police officer candidate in a city training academy was $6,500, a figure that has probably more than doubled due to inflation and to generally larger training periods over the past decade. In Memphis, police officials estimate that the total cost for recruitment, selection, and training for a period of 18 weeks is $18,000. However, even after the rookie is commissioned, there is a great likelihood that as a rookie he or she will be unable to work with the efficiency and compe- tency of the street-wise veteran he or she replaced. Finally, voluntary resignations of experienced officers may help to create a climate in which other officers begin to question their choice of an occupation, with a resultant weakening of morale and esprit de corps.

Voluntary resignations of police officers are also noteworthy when placed in context of the occupation. Becoming a police officer is often seen as a "calling" to a tremendously important service that is inherently interesting and exciting, attracting a special and committed breed of largely working-class young people who are security conscious and who remain in the service to retirement (Niederhoffer, 1967). Another notable aspect of policing is the fraternal character of the occupation. Because of the constabulary role that every police officer experiences, strong sub- cultural ties are generated, and policing becomes a tightly knit fraternity, unlike most other occupational groupings (Skolnick, 1975).

This dedication to a calling, the occupational security, and the encul- turation process that generates strong subcultural ties to the occupation would lead to the hypothesis that police officers are bound to the occupation very strongly. Consequently, one would conclude that volun- tary resignations of commissions would be a difficult occupational choice made only for very serious reasons.

One explanation of police turnover focuses on problems of adjustment which new officers experience as their ideals of service and academy training conflict with the reality of police work "in the streets." The new officer may experience cognitive dissonance (Festinger, 1957), a psycho- logically painful experience that occurs when the officer has contradictory perceptions or beliefs about his or her role as a police officer (Skolnick, 1975; Westley, 1956; McDonnell 1971). This cognitive dissonance moti- vates the officer to reduce the psychological conflict by either changing parts of his knowledge system, allowing him to continue in the police officer role, or leaving the police department, allowing the officer's ideal- ized model of police work to remain intact. This theoretical position may explain turnover among officers within their first few months or years of service but does not satisfactorily explain resignations of more experienced officers. It seems that the more experienced officers with several years of service would have resolved the dissonance between the ideal and the real at earlier stages of their careers.

A second theoretical orientation currently in vogue postulates that officers leave police work because of burnout due to stresses of the job (Kroes et al., 1974; Hillgren et al., 1976; Reiser, 1974). While this hypothesis may logically point to the danger inherent in police work as a primary source of stress, two studies (Kroes et al., 1974; Singleton and Teahan, 1978) did not find danger to be a primary stressor. Such factors as departmental management style, court policies, community expectations, actions of city officials, and organizational policies have been found to be major sources of stress for police officers. Management style was identified by Reiser (1974) as a major source of stress, particularly the traditional, authoritarian style. He also found other stressors to be a lack of opportunity for fulfillment of self-actualization and ego needs, the internal discipline structure, and peer group influence. Jirak (1975) found that the subjects of his study (551 police officers on New York's Staten Island) felt a sense of alienation from the community and were high in feelings of normlessness. He also found that feelings of alienation increased with years of service.

It appears unlikely that a particularly stressful event or a specific episode of danger causes burnout and subsequent resignation from the department. When these stressful variables operate, they are more likely to be viewed as pernicious sources of dissatisfaction whose effects are more likely to be continuous and cumulative. Since the effect of stress and/or dissatisfaction in police work is likely to be relatively constant and apparent to the neophyte shortly after joining the force (Van Maanen, 1975), the logical assumption is that there exists a triggering mechanism which alerts the officer to the reality of his particular situation, to the likelihood that significant job factors will change, and which accounts for an officer finally deciding that he should change occupations.

One can assume that any occupation or organization will possess factors, possibly idiosyncratic to that occupation or organization, which are dissatisfiers to those who work therein. It seems logical to conclude, therefore, that these sources of dissatisfaction will exert some stressful impact on workers. This study will attempt to identify particular sources of dissatisfaction among police officers who have voluntarily resigned their commissions. Second, the authors will attempt to identify "turning points" when the decision to leave police work was made. Lofland (1966: 50-51) has used the concept of turning points to indicate "a moment when old lines of action were complete, had failed, or had been or were about to be disrupted, and when they were faced with the opportunity or necessity for doing something different with their lives. . . . The significance of these various kinds of turning points lies in their having produced an increased awareness of and desire to take some action on their problems, combined with a new opportunity to do so. Turning points were circumstances in which new involvements had become desired and possible." Our working hypothesis is that sources of dissatisfaction in the police agency create stress among police officers, a process that serves to raise their consciousness about the likelihood of these sources of dissatisfaction dissipating and creating a psychological state of readiness to conduct a reevaluation of their career possibilities. In order to reduce this stress, accommodations to the job will be made that will result in reduced involvement in the police officer role (Van Maanen, 1975) or the officer will voluntarily resign from police work. Our effort will be to explain the voluntary resignations from the standpoint of the officers having reached a "turning point" in their lives and careers.

METHODOLOGY

The study was conducted in Memphis, Tennessee, a relatively large city (population 650,000) on the Mississippi River in the southwestern corner of the state. The Memphis Police Department has an authorized strength of 1,243 sworn personnel and has experienced a considerable amount of labor unrest during the past decade. These tensions reached their apex in 1978 and culminated in a strike of police officers in the ranks of patrolman and sergeant, a nonsupervisory rank in the Memphis Police Department (see Giacopassi and Sparger, 1981). As in many departments, the department and city officials were concerned about this labor unrest and with the significant loss of qualified personnel, and they consented to permit a study that sought the reason for the voluntary resignations. Questionnaires were constructed that contained both open-ended and Likert-scale items in an effort to determine the reasons for this voluntary attrition.

The questionnaires were mailed to all personnel who had voluntarily terminated their commissions in the Memphis Police Department between July 1, 1975, and June 30, 1980. None of the respondents had completed sufficient service to qualify for retirement from the Memphis Police Department. There were 153 persons identified as potential respondents, and accurate addresses were obtained for 123 persons. From these 123 potential respondents, 25 of the questionnaires were returned as a result of the initial mailing. Six weeks later, a follow-up letter and questionnaire were mailed, which netted an additional 33 responses. A total of 58 responses were obtained for a response rate of 47 percent. While this response rate falls short of what the authors expected and desired, the nature of the study and the fact that the respondents had been absent from policing for a period of from one to five years, had assumed and become invested in other careers, and had possibly lost interest in the problems of their former employer makes even this response rate greater than one might reasonably expect. While there are no data available on nonrespondents, the authors cannot find compelling reason to assume that they differ significantly on any dimension from the respondents in the study.

Of the respondents, 85 percent were white, and 88 percent were males. Their average age was 33.5, and their average length of service was 6.9 years in the department. The mean educational attainment was 15.0 years, and 91 percent were in the rank of patrolman when they terminated their employment.

ANALYSIS OF THE DATA

In order to determine the sources of dissatisfaction experienced by the respondents to the study, a priori assumptions were made by the authors based on informal discussions with police personnel that the following items would address most of these factors: departmental politics, lack of opportunity for promotion, departmental corruption, no opportunity to have a voice in departmental policy, inadequate pay and fringe benefits, feeling that efforts to do a good job were not appreciated, feeling of isolation from persons outside the department, union activities, police strike, family problems, frustration over judicial and court policies, and feeling that efforts really did not matter. A category of "other (please specify)" was included so that the respondents could identify sources of dissatisfaction that the authors might have overlooked or that might have been idiosyncratic to the respondent(s).

The respondents were presented with these items in the questionnaire and asked to rate them using a 5-point Likert scale with a rating of 1 representing "no cause of dissatisfaction" and a rating of 5 representing "a very great cause of dissatisfaction," to indicate how each item contributed to the dissatisfaction the respondent experienced as a police officer. After the respondents had rated each item, they were asked to select the three most important causes of dissatisfaction and to rank them in order of their importance.

Using the data from the respondents' ratings of each source of dissatisfaction, a mean rating of each item was calculated (sum of ratings ÷ number rating each item). In order to determine the importance of each item as a source of dissatisfaction, the rankings of the items were assigned weights (a ranking of 1 was assigned a weight of 4, a ranking of 2 was assigned a weight of 3, a ranking of 3 was assigned a weight of 2, and no ranking was assigned a weight of 1). For each item, the weighted ranking was obtained by multiplying the mean rating of the item by the frequency (fr) of respondents ranking the item 1, 2, or 3, times the weight for each ranking, as in the following diagram or formula: $(\bar{X}item \times fr_1 \times W_4 + \bar{X}item \times fr_2 \times W_3 + \bar{X}item \times fr_3 \times W_2 + \bar{X}item \times fnr \times W_1 / N)$. The weighted rankings for the causes of dissatisfaction among the respondents in this study are shown in Table 5.1.

From the table it can be seen that the primary sources of dissatisfaction of these respondents are a perceived lack of opportunity for promotion within the department (8.07) and departmental politics (7.00). Of slightly less importance in the respondents' views are feelings that their efforts were not appreciated (5.56) and pay and fringe benefits (5.28). Following closely behind pay and fringe benefits as a source of dissatisfaction is the feeling that one's efforts did not matter (4.69), either in obtaining the rewards of the department or in accomplishing the goals of the organization. The remainder of the causes of dissatisfaction appear to cluster together with the police strike (3.74), no voice in departmental policy (3.53), departmental corruption (3.41), judicial and court policies (3.29), and union activities (3.11) appearing to have little significant difference as sources of dissatisfaction among the respondents. The factors of isolation from the community (2.51) and family problems (2.13) appear to be almost insignificant as sources of dissatisfaction due to their low ranking and the fact that only 2 respondents ranked isolation from the community and only 5 persons ranked family problems 1, 2, or 3 as causes of dissatisfaction.

However interesting or revealing these data are regarding dissatisfaction with this particular department, the data do not reveal an explanation for why our respondents chose to resign their commissions. In an effort at explanation, we chose to examine other data to attempt to determine what factors are important to the decision to leave police work. It appears that dissatisfaction is a necessary but not sufficient condition to cause

TABLE 5.1 Causes of Dissatisfaction

Variable	Frequency No. 1	Frequency No. 2	Frequency No. 3	Number Ranking	Weighted Ranking
Lack of promotion opportunity	10	11	7	28	8.07
Departmental politics	9	7	9	25	7.00
Efforts not appreciated	3	4	10	17	5.56
Pay and fringe benefits	7	6	5	18	5.28
Feeling efforts did not matter	2	5	3	10	4.69
Police strike	5	2	3	10	3.74
No voice in dept. policy	0	2	4	6	3.53
Departmental corruption	3	2	4	6	3.41
Judicial & court policies	2	3	1	6	3.29
Union activities	1	5	1	7	3.11
Isolation from community	0	2	0	2	2.51
Family problems	2	0	3	5	2.13

resignation, because it seems that many police officers who may be equally dissatisfied over the same factors do not resign. Perhaps to understand why resignations occur, the dissatisfiers must be examined through the cognitive lenses of the individual officer; that is, each must be placed in the context of the individual's subjective universe. As Muchinsky and Morrow (1980: 267) have stated, "The appropriate unit of analysis is the individual, not a collectivity such as a work group or organization. While individual turnover data can be aggregated to produce turnover rates for organizational subunits, and these organizational subunits may be contrasted via differences in employee turnover, turnover is initially an individual phenomenon."

Cross (1977) has utilized the concept of "turning points" to explain why people become police officers. The three most prevalent turning points that he identified were stagnation in the old job, age (passing the minimum or approaching the maximum age allowed for entering police work), and new opportunity (graduating from or leaving school or separation from military service). He concluded:

> . . . simply because a person passes through a turning point and becomes a policeman does not mean the individual will be locked into the police occupation. There is no distinct point where a person adopts a role and forever remains tied to it. Policemen, like individuals in other occupations, may become disillusioned with or grow out of their occupations. Becoming a policeman not only involves a problematic process of entrance, but also involves a continual adjustment to the job and to one's social relationships once the occupation has been entered. A person might join and then quit police work when he had a better avenue of opportunity open to him—therefore leading to another turning point in his life [Cross, 1977: 164].

Using this concept, we looked at the answers to open-ended questions designed to determine the ex-officers' reasons for their resigning in an effort to find common response sets. As with the Cross (1977) study, it was possible to identify turning points for all 58 respondents. The seven turning points identified and the percent of respondents in each category are presented in Table 5.2.

It should be stressed that the turning points are not mutually exclusive categories. It was not unusual for a respondent to present a list of reasons for resigning. Judgments had to be made based on the emphasis provided by the respondent's answers as to which turning point was most decisive in that particular individual's decision-making process. It should also be

TABLE 5.2   Turning Points

	Respondents	*Percentage*
Stagnation-no opportunity for advancement	30	51.7
Intense experience	7	12.1
Lack of self-fulfillment	6	10.3
Family considerations	5	8.6
Unprofessional attitudes of co-workers	4	6.9
Official department policies	4	6.9
New opportunities	2	3.5
	58	100.0

noted that while the seven turning points identified are exhaustive for the population studied, other studies of other departments might well reveal other turning points.

STAGNATION

By far, the most common reason given for resignation was the feeling of stagnating in one's job. Of the 58 respondents, 30 (51.7 percent) resigned because of this factor. Many of the ex-officers at the time of their resignations were at the stage of their law enforcement careers where they expected and believed they deserved promotion. When promotions were neither forthcoming nor anticipated, hopelessness and frustration developed. This turning point is illustrated by the responses to the question, "What was the single most important reason you left the Memphis Police Department?"

- *36-year-old white male, 12-year veteran:* "I felt that my career of 12½ years was on the track of a 25-year patrolman."

- *37-year-old black male, 11-year veteran:* "I just can't see any future in being a police officer."

- *31-year-old white male, 4-year veteran:* "Almost total lack of incentive and a feeling of being trapped in a particular job."

- *34-year-old white male, 2-year veteran:* There was no chance for advancement based on infrequent promotions.

Many of those who felt they were stagnating focused their displeasure on the promotion and evaluation process. These officers typically blamed arbitrary promotion and evaluation policies, poorly trained supervisors, and department politics for their plight. Examples of this response set include the following:

- *34-year-old white female, 5-year veteran:* "Unfortunately you are not promoted for your wisdom, tact, ability, or leadership. You are generally promoted because you play their games and know the right people. No matter how well you accomplish your duties and how dedicated you were to the department, the person beside you could goof off and transact personal business all day and get paid the same amount. Probably he could get promoted if he played his cards right with the right people in the administration."

- *34-year-old white male, 7-year veteran:* "The police department is a who you know system, or a whose rear end you are willing to smack to get ahead."

- *42-year-old white male, 13-year veteran:* "Politics. Even though I was number one in nearly every category (apprehensions, recovery of stolen property, etc.) in my unit, I was made aware of the fact that I backed the wrong candidate for a political office. Hard work and dedication does not get you ahead. It's what team you are on."

Included in the stagnation category were four respondents (6.9 percent) who listed economic stagnation as their prime reason for resigning. While patrol officers receive approximately the same salary, relative few experience salary as a turning point. Yet, as Lofland (1966) wrote, it is the subjective experience of increased awareness that constitutes a turning point. A 32-year-old white male who was a 7-year veteran of the force responded to the question, "Was there a significant change in your financial condition just prior to your leaving the department?" by stating emphatically "Yes": "Everything was higher except the pay raises." A 33-year-old white male, 6-year veteran, responded similarly: "The buying power of my income was greatly diminished by inflation." Both of these individuals perceived an ongoing circumstance (low pay) as a deteriorating crisis situation.

INTENSE EXPERIENCE

The second most common turning point was experiencing an intense situation that convinced the individual he should resign from the force. Of the seven persons in this category, only one resigned because of a violent episode. In this instance the individual was injured, felt he could no longer perform his duties adequately, and did not desire a "desk job." Two resigned because they felt themselves placed in an untenable position by some of their colleagues who were violating the law. The most commonly mentioned experience leading to resignation was the 1978 Memphis police strike that lasted for eight days. Four officers resigned as a direct result of the strike.

- *27-year-old white male, 5-year veteran:* "I was one of the four patrolmen who remained on duty from the very beginning of the strike. How can a man of conscience remain where the people responsible for public safety will fully betray their public trust? It would be most difficult to work for a man over the next 15-20 years who'd been a striker and respect him. The strikers will never forget the faithful and the faithful will never forget the strikers."

- *31-year-old white male, 6-year veteran:* "Frustrations had built up over a period of time. Then with the despicable conditions after the strike plus two partners who were closer than brothers leaving put a cap on it."

LACK OF FULFILLMENT

The third most prevalent turning point was lack of self-fulfillment. While only 4.3 percent of the respondents in the Cross (1977) study left their old jobs and became police officers seeking more self-fulfillment, the present study shows 10.3 percent leaving police work to seek a more fulfilling job. Intertwined with lack of fulfillment was a sense of frustration that nothing was being accomplished. Examples of these sentiments are evident from responses given to the question, "What did you like least about police work?"

- *32-year-old white male, 6-year veteran:* "Being exposed to the sadness and problems of others and not being able to help . . ."

- *32-year-old white male, 6-year veteran:* "Frustration with the whole system had reached the limit."

- *38-year-old black female, 6-year veteran:* "A realization that I would never be able to work with the sex crime victims I had joined the department to attempt to assist."

- 37-year-old white male, 12-year veteran: "The feeling that I was caught in the middle between the scum and the judicial system. I thought very often that I, and not the crook, was the one on trial."

FAMILY

Family considerations were the fourth most prevalent turning point. Of the five respondents (8.6 percent) in this category, two were female. One left to help her husband in business; the other left to be married. Only one male respondent mentioned marital problems as the reason he left the police department. More typical male responses were phrased in terms of the individual's wish to better the family's lot.

- *37-year-old white male, 8-year veteran:* "I wanted a better life for my family."

- *33-year-old white male, 6-year veteran:* "To better the educational advantages of my children."

CONDUCT OF CO-WORKERS

Unprofessional attitudes of co-workers and official department policies were the next most commonly mentioned turning points, each being characteristic of four respondents (6.9 percent of the total).

Comments of the four respondents who found cause to resign in the unprofessional conduct of other officers generally contained a dual complaint. Most expressed pride at being police officers and found it difficult to resolve their pride with the public's tendency to condemn all police officers for the actions of a few. They not only felt that this condemnation made their job harder to accomplish but also that their personal reputations were being tarnished. The second source of complaint focused on the lack of reliability of some of those with whom they worked. Once again, answers to the question, "What did you like least about being a police officer?" illustrate these points.

- *36-year-old black male, 6-year veteran:* "Having to live down misconceptions and stereotypes that the community has of police."

- *32-year-old white male, 4-year veteran:* "Unprofessional manners of my fellow officers. Also the lack of devotion to duty. It is true that the money I made as an officer was inadequate, but that wasn't why I quit. I felt that no matter how hard I tried to do my job, I was going backwards. I was out there risking my life for a paycheck with no thanks, while others were out there doing nothing for the same check and getting away with almost anything they wanted to. It was at the point where you couldn't trust or rely on the partner you worked with."

- *34-year-old white male, 7-year veteran:* "Because of other patrolmen embarrassing the department and fellow officers—bad attitudes and lack of dependability from some fellow officers."

DEPARTMENT POLICY

Official department policy was also mentioned as a turning point by four respondents. Only one respondent mentioned the strict rules and discipline often thought characteristic of law enforcement agencies.

- *37-year-old black male, 11-year veteran:* "I wanted to live by my own rules without being dictated to 24 hours a day. I felt my life belonged to me and not the city."

More common were complaints directed at work regulations.

- *31-year-old white male, 5-year veteran:* "Upon entering my fifth year on the force I realized that no matter how hard I had worked that I was in a position where no advancement could be seen because of a bidding system where it took 10 years to even be able to change assignments."
- *37-year-old male, 10-year veteran:* "Seniority bid system for job transfer, fixed shifts, promotion policy is too subjective."

NEW OPPORTUNITY

The least common turning point was new avenues of opportunity presenting themselves. In the Cross (1977) study, this factor was characteristic of 15.7 percent of the respondents. Most were becoming police officers after leaving college or having been discharged from military service. Of the 58 respondents leaving police work, only two (3.5 percent) were similarly classified. Of these, one joined the ministry and the other left the department to study for a law degree.

- *27-year-old white male, 6-year veteran:* "Law school provided an opportunity to leave the department. Many other officers would resign if they had the financial opportunity."

SUMMARY AND CONCLUSIONS

The respondents in this study indicated that their primary sources of dissatisfaction in their work as police officers were a lack of opportunity for advancement, departmental politics, a lack of appreciation for their efforts, pay and fringe benefits, and a feeling that their efforts did not matter, either in obtaining the rewards of the department or in accomplishing the goals of the organization. Of lesser consequence appear to be factors of the police strike, participation in policy formulation, departmental corruption, judical and court policies, and union activities. The factors of isolation from the community and family problems do not seem to be significant sources of dissatisfaction.

Seven turning points were identified as detailing the events and emotions that led to the voluntary resignations of these police officers. These turning points are job stagnation, intense experience, lack of self-fulfillment, family considerations, unprofessional attitudes of co-workers, official departmental policies, and new opportunities.

Our analysis indicates that there is a positive relationship between sources of dissatisfaction and the expressed reasons given for quitting. As Muchinsky and Morrow (1980: 271) have noted, "An extensive body of research has shown that job satisfaction is indexed by satisfaction with work itself. Furthermore, employed workers seeking alternate employment . . . indicate that their search is motivated by dissatisfaction with some aspect(s) of their current job." As dissatisfiers, lack of promotion opportunity and departmental politics (on which promotion is perceived as dependent) were ranked 1 and 2 respectively, while 51.7 percent of the respondents indicated that "stagnation—no opportunity for advancement" was their primary consideration in terminating their employment. Reiss (1967) has identified lack of promotional opportunities and promotional policies that are erratic and unpredictable as the primary sources of dissatisfaction in major metropolitan police departments. A feeling that one's efforts were not appreciated and feeling that one's efforts did not matter ranked 3 and 5 respectively as sources of dissatisfaction, while 10.3 percent of the respondents indicated that lack of self-fulfillment was their reason for leaving police work.

Surprisingly, pay and fringe benefits do not seem to be a paramount factor causing officers to quit. While many respondents indicated that this factor was a source of dissatisfaction (ranking third), and while many of them expressed displeasure over salary levels, only a small percentage (6.9) listed inadequate pay as the prime motive for seeking new employment.

Muchinsky and Morrow (1980: 266) state, "We are of the opinion that economic factors may add appreciably to our understanding of turnover. We do not view the antecedents of turnover as being an either/or phenomenon, either psychological or economic in nature. Both sets of factors contribute to the turnover process, although the impact of economic factors may be greater than many psychologists have cared to consider." We note that economic factors are seen as a prominent source of dissatisfaction but not a critical factor in the decision to terminate employment by our respondents.

While much has been made of the impact of police work on family life, family pressures reportedly were a relatively unimportant factor in causing officers to quit. Also, while having an intense job-related experience was the second most commonly indicated turning point, the experiences were not the violently traumatic ones generally believed significant.

DISCUSSION

Our analysis of why these police officers have voluntarily resigned their commissions indicates that most do not resign for extraordinary reasons experienced only by police officers. Rather, they share the same occupational dissatisfactions, frustrations, and concerns as do nonpolice personnel, which culminate in a turning point when they perceive that a change is not only possible but also desirable (see Muchinsky and Morrow, 1980).

The turning points identified cast doubt on some of the traditional ideas relative to police labor turnover. Pay was not among the major factors causing officers to quit, nor was pay the paramount cause of dissatisfaction. While many of the respondents expressed dissatisfaction over salary levels, only a small proportion listed inadequate pay as the prime motive for seeking new employment. Similarly, family pressures reportedly were a minor source of dissatisfaction and relatively unimportant in causing officers to quit. While having an intense job-related experience was the second most common turning point, the intense experiences were not the violently traumatic ones generally believed significant.

The present study found that the most common of the turning points is the same one Cross (1977) found most prevalent in his study of why persons left old jobs to become police officers—the feeling of stagnation in one's job with little hope of future betterment. This turning point and dissatisfier is apparently not idiosyncratic with the department studied (Reiss, 1967).

While the ex-officers generally expressed frustration over the routine of police work, it is important to note that many did not dislike the job, as evidenced by the extraordinary fact that 21 of the 58 respondents (36 percent) made unsolicited comments expressing regrets over leaving police work. What these officers sought was the opportunity for professional growth and advancement (see Swanson, 1977). Not finding this opportunity in police work, they turned elsewhere in an effort to satisfy this need.

This discussion of the basic reasons for police officers leaving the occupation presents complex issues that must be addressed by police administrators. Dramatic changes have occurred in the composition of personnel entering police organizations: Not only have the more educated citizenry been recruited, but more women, blacks, and other minority groups represent important groupings within police departments. Each of these groups has unique needs and concerns that must be recognized and met if the occupation is to retain its members. Increased workloads assumed by police officers, the increased questioning of authority in our society, and a greater demand for stricter political accountability have served to create an unsettled organizational climate confounding the problem of retention of officers. Coupling these factors with the findings of the present study, we might hypothesize that new recruits entering the police organization have greater abilities and expectations than those whose careers began in an earlier era, yet there are more impediments to realizing these expectations.

Those concerned with voluntary attrition in police agencies might note that the average age of the respondents was 33 years, and the mean level of experience in police work was 6.9 years. Several studies of police personnel indicate that officers experience an occupational crisis in this time frame (Niederhoffer, 1967; Lotz and Regoli, 1977; Regoli and Poole, 1978). Additionally, it should be noted that the mean educational level of the respondents was 15 years. It seems logical that persons with these qualities, and who have no record of misconduct, would be the type of persons police agencies would want to retain.

To accomplish the goal of retaining those police officers who have met the heightened entrance standards that police agencies have set over the past decade, several policy issues might be considered. First, the police administrator might consider the need to dispel, at the recruitment stage, the romanticized media myths of policing by providing the applicant with a realistic picture of what can be expected in the police officer role. Second, the applicant might be apprised of the fact that comparatively few personnel are needed in supervisory and command positions relative to the total number of personnel in a police department. Therefore, many competent and qualified officers will, of necessity, remain in the field with few, if any, supervisory or administrative responsibilities. While this approach might discourage some qualified applicants from entering police work, providing the applicant with this cogent information could possibly diminish future dissatisfaction and lower the rate of turnover among those who choose the occupation after being forewarned of the exigencies of the organization.

While the implementation of these policies might serve to disabuse the neophyte police officer of unrealistic expectations of police service and promote greater organizational stability, they will not address issues that more experienced officers view as fatal flaws in the organization (such as departmental politics, promotion opportunity, career stagnation, unappreciated and ineffective effort). Our findings suggest that police administrators might focus on the development of valid and objective performance evaluation and promotion procedures for providing relevant feedback, dispensation of rewards, and nonpolitical selection of supervisory and command personnel. Further, the incorporation of a career development program within the organization, in addition to this program's traditional elements, might include such factors as rotation of assignment throughout the department's subcomponents so that an officer might learn how the subcomponents operate and for which area one is most suited in mapping out a career. This approach might serve also to increase appreciation among the rank-and-file of the dilemmas of management within a political bureaucracy and assist in the identification and development of those with management potential.

Based on the findings of this study, the authors are led to hypothesize that those persons who choose to leave police work for another occupation may, on the average, enter police work at a later age, have more years of higher education, have a greater need for personal achievement, be more likely to take risks, be less concerned with job security, and have less organizational commitment than their former colleagues. In the absence of a comparison group of police officers, equated for date of entry and length of service, we can only speculate about these factors as discriminating variables with explanatory power. However, since we believe that turnover is an important issue, these factors deserve further study if police agencies are to take corrective action in an effort to retain currently and potentially valuable employees.

REFERENCES

CROSS, S. (1977) "Turning points: an alternative view of becoming a policeman." Journal of Police Science and Administration 5: 155-164.

FESTINGER, L. (1957) A Theory of Cognitive Dissonance. Evanston, IL: Row-Peterson.

GIACOPASSI, D. and J. R. SPARGER (1981) "The Memphis police strike: a retrospective analysis." Southern Journal of Criminal Justice 6: 39-52.

HILLGREN, J., S. JONES, and R. BOND (1976) "Primary stressors in police administration and law enforcement." Journal of Police Science and Administration 4: 445-449.

JIRAK, M. (1975) "Alienation among members of the New York city police department on Staten Island." Journal of Police Science and Administration 3: 149-159.

KROES, W., B. MARGOLIS, and J. HURRELL, Jr. (1974) "Job stress in policemen." Journal of Police Science and Administration 2: 145-155.

LOFLAND, J. (1966) Doomsday Cult. Englewood Cliffs, NJ: Prentice-Hall.

LOTZ, R. and R. REGOLI (1977) "Police cynicism and professionalism." Human Relations 30: 175-186.

McDONNELL, C. (1971) "The police as victims of their own misconception." Journal of Criminal Law, Criminology and Police Science 62: 431-438.

MUCHINSKY, P. and P. MORROW (1980) "Multidisciplinary model of voluntary employee turnover." Journal of Vocational Behavior 17: 263-290.

National Advisory Commission on Criminal Justice Standards and Goals (1973) Police. Washington, DC: U.S. Government Printing Office.

NIEDERHOFFER, A. (1967) Behind the Shield: The Police in Urban Society. Garden City, NY: Doubleday.

REGOLI, R. and E. POOLE (1978) "Specifying police cynicism." Journal of Police Science and Administration 6: 98-104.

REGOLI, R., E. POOLE, and J. HEWITT (1979) "Exploring the empirical relationship between police cynicism and work alienation." Journal of Police Science and Administration 7: 336-340.

REISER, M. (1974) "Some organizational stresses on policeman." Journal of Police Science and Administration 2: 156-159.

REISS, A. (1967) Studies of Crime and Law Enforcement in Major Metropolitan Areas, 2. Washington, DC: U.S. Government Printing Office.

SINGLETON, G. and J. TEHAN (1978) "Effects of job-related stress on the physical and psychological adjustment of police officers." Journal of Police Science and Administration 6: 355-361.

SKOLNICK, J. (1975) Justice Without Trial: Law Enforcement in a Democratic Society. New York: John Wiley.

SWANSON, C. (1977) "An uneasy look at college education and the police organization." Journal of Criminal Justice 5: 311-320.

WESTLEY, J. (1956) "Secrecy and the police." Social Forces 34: 254-257.

VAN MAANEN, J. (1975) "Police socialization: a longitudinal examination of job attitudes in an urban police department." Administrative Science Quarterly 20: 207-227.

III.

Police and the Community

The expression "to protect and serve," which has been the police establishment's byword regarding its relationship with the community, will take on new meaning in the police research and analysis of the 1980s. While the expression has traditionally described the services the police render to the community, in the 1980s it will direct attention to the police working environment and the *process* by which these services are selected, prioritized, and delivered. In addition, the 1980s will see more research focusing on the linkage between the community and the police working environment.

The two chapters presented in Part III address this linkage. Scott and Percy investigated the gatekeeping function of police operators and dispatchers, who stand between police officers and the community they serve. These intermediaries influence both groups. The vast majority of calls for police service originate within the community, and by their actions the gatekeepers determine what and when police services are rendered. Their functions include (1) determining the eligibility of requests for service, (2) matching each eligible request with a type of response, (3) selecting the appropriate form of police response, and (4) coordinating the response. The authors also document how gatekeepers influence the police working environment by determining officer workload, the speed and priority of calls, and the type and quantity of information given to the responding officers. Although the authors insist that their study is exploratory, the policy implications apparent in their work are important. The gatekeepers constitute a powerful organizational unit that can reinforce or undermine formal department policies vis-à-vis the community. Their training and supervision should be conducted with this in mind. Further policy research should focus on gaining greater understanding of their actual and potential roles.

The second selection, by Cordner, Greene, and Bynum, also advances our understanding of calls for service, gatekeeping, and the delivery of police services in the community. While the study may at first glance appear to be a standard investigation of police response time, the authors adroitly expand their focus to include community influences on response time. In addition to the traditional measures of response outcome, such as arrest, the authors employ solvability factors and levels of investigation follow-up. Although limited by weak correlation coefficients, the study supports Scott and Percy's call for further policy research to understand better the role of the dispatcher and other gatekeepers who influence the quality of the police-community linkage. The study also suggests that policies regarding differentiation among police calls for service should attempt to make the most effective use of resources in the police working environment. Both selections demonstrate that policy research and analysis in the 1980s must look to the partnership between the community and the police for the potential resolution of crime and crime-related problems.

6.

GATEKEEPING POLICE SERVICES:
Police Operators and Dispatchers

Eric J. Scott
Stephen L. Percy
Indiana University

Contemporary analysts of public service provision stress the prevalence and importance of discretion in the job functions of service delivery agents. Michael Lipsky (1980) has developed the concept of the "street-level bureaucrat," which recognizes that public officers who deliver services through face-to-face interactions with citizens operate with substantial discretion. While discretion in service delivery is not a new phenomenon, widespread recognition of its extensiveness and importance is relatively recent.

The role of discretion in service delivery has been noted frequently with reference to police services. As Goldstein (1977: 93) states:

> In the past the prevalent assumption of both the police and the public was that the police had no discretion—that their job was to function in strict accordance with the law. . . . But behind this facade, in sub-rosa fashion and with an air of illegitimacy, the police have, of necessity, functioned in a much looser and more informal manner—making frequent choices and exercising broad discretion in order to carry out their multiple responsibilities.

Authors' Note: *This chapter has been prepared as part of a research project that is examining demand processing and information flow in police agencies. The project, conducted at the Workshop in Political Theory and Policy Analysis at Indiana*

We now openly recognize that police personnel possess and frequently use discretion in the course of daily service delivery activities. We have also become aware that the exercise of this discretion can have profound impact on the quality of services delivered.

As Goldstein (1977) correctly points out, we are still working through the many problems, constraints, and opportunities that arise from the existence of discretion. Some efforts have been made to analyze discretion in the broad context of policing and the criminal justice system (see, for example, J. Goldstein, 1960; H. Goldstein, 1977; LaFave, 1962a, 1962b; Parnas, 1971; Kadish, 1962; Abernathy, 1962). Other analyses have considered the widespread nature of patrol officer discretion and have speculated on its causes, consequences, and legal implications (Goldstein, 1977; Manning, 1977; Pepinsky, 1975; Rubinstein, 1973; Reiss, 1971; Silberman, 1978; Wilson, 1968).

While recognition of discretion in policing has been growing, only limited attention has been paid to its existence and effects in the job tasks of police telephone operators and dispatchers. But these personnel play crucial roles in formulating police response to calls for service. Police operators act as gatekeepers; they mediate initial agency interaction with citizens demanding service and assess caller eligibility and the exact nature of the service request. Dispatchers are response coordinators, determining the specifics of police response and communicating relevant information to patrol officers. The purpose of this article is to explore police discretion in the important functions of gatekeeping and response coordination, that is, in the work tasks of police telephone operators and dispatchers. After considering the concept and practice of discretion, we speculate about the impact of operator and dispatcher discretion on police performance.

THE CONCEPT OF DISCRETION

Discretion broadly connotes the idea that public officials, whether administrators or street-level bureaucrats, can make decisions and take actions that are not totally constrained by organizational rules and procedures. That is, officials have some degree of choice when taking actions. In writing about discretion, several authors have used the definition

University, is funded by Grant 80-IJ-AX-0020 from the National Institute of Justice. The authors gratefully acknowledge this research support. We wish to thank Richard Bennett, Joan Luxenburg, Douglas Smith, Rick K. Wilson, and three anonymous referees for comments made on earlier versions of this chapter.

offered by Kenneth Davis (1969: 4): "A public officer has discretion whenever the effective limits on his power leave him free to make a choice among possible courses of action and inaction." Davis notes that his definition includes both cases of legal and illegal discretion. He also includes the notion of "inaction," arguing that not taking action is often a significant decision option with important consequences.

Discretion implies freedom to make decisions about action or inaction. Limitations on discretionary action stem from two sources. The first is official rules and regulations that prescribe what "should" be done in various service delivery situations. Rules and regulations derive from several sources, including legislative action, court decisions, constitutional rights and guarantees, and administrative decisions. Police personnel, for example, are at least nominally governed by rules concerning a whole range of activities, including gathering evidence, making arrests, and deciding whether to send a police unit in response to a call for service.

A system of enforcement that provides sanctions and incentives to officials to follow prescribed rules and procedures is the second check on discretion. Rules and regulations alone are unlikely to limit discretionary decision making; to be effective, they must be accompanied by enforcement mechanisms. The degree to which such mechanisms can bound discretion is a function of several factors, including the comprehensiveness and specificity of rules, the severity of sanctions and reward of incentives, and the degree of oversight and supervision.

Although it may be possible to limit discretionary actions of public officials including police—indeed, some, like Davis (1969) and Goldstein (1977), recommend this—it is unlikely that discretion can ever be completely eliminated from the work tasks of service delivery agents. Discretion will remain an integral component of public service delivery because of the complexity of human needs and situations, the inability or unwillingness of legislators and administrators to define comprehensive rules about service delivery, and the need for individualized responses to complex problems (Lipsky, 1980; Davis, 1969).

DISCRETION IN POLICE GATEKEEPING

Gatekeeping refers to boundary spanning activities through which service agencies like police receive and interpret requests for service and initiate or refuse organization response. In police departments, the gatekeeping function is performed by telephone operators, or call takers, who receive and process requests for service. Police call takers perform a variety of tasks, including (1) determination of eligibility of service requests; (2) interpretation, coding, and transmission of demand messages; (3) selection of initial response alternatives; and (4) provision of information to persons requesting services.

A substantial amount of police activity stems directly from citizen calls for service. Black (1970) reported that more than three-fourths of all police-citizen encounters were initiated by telephone.[1] Call takers are the first officials with whom most people requesting police service interact. The initial decisions of police phone operators determine much of what occurs in the department on a routine, day-to-day basis. Determining which callers are eligible for service, coding incidents into agency-relevant terminology, selecting the appropriate form of response, and communicating demand and response information to the caller are important decisions that significantly affect police performance and citizen perceptions and evaluations. Operators must make these decisions rapidly and repeatedly, often without guidance from rules and in the absence of supervision. The consequences of the discretionary decisions of police gatekeepers can be far-reaching for both citizens and the police.

Determination of Eligibility

The first call taker task, determining eligibility, involves evaluating incoming service requests in terms of a variety of criteria governing access to services. There is probably less discretion in determining eligibility for police services than for other social services such as welfare. Criteria used in determining eligibility are varied but commonly include geographic boundaries, service domain, and seriousness of need. Police call takers generally have little discretion when judging eligibility in terms of geographic boundaries. If the problem or crime reported by the caller occurs outside a department's jurisdiction, almost universally that caller will be denied access to service. He or she is often provided information about or referred to other sources of information or assistance, however.

A second set of eligibility requirements relates to an agency's service domain, or the set of services that it considers a part of its legitimate responsibility. The service domain of most police agencies is normally quite broad, recognizing as legitimate most requests for service associated with crime, medical or other emergencies, disturbances, suspicious persons or circumstances, traffic accidents and problems, and a variety of other social problems. The breadth of the police service domain is one source of gatekeeper discretion. While call takers generally judge most service requests related to crime and victimization as appropriate for police response, they have more latitude in rejecting requests for general assistance and social services. Consider the case of a minor noise disturbance. Some call takers might accept this as a legitimate request, while others, especially during peak demand periods, might judge the noise problem as inappropriate for police response.

A third group of eligibility requirements is related to the immediacy and seriousness of need associated with the service request. Operators are much more likely to consider demands for emergency assistance as eligible for police response than they are requests for assistance in minor problems, such as noisy children playing nearby. It is often difficult to determine the extent of human need, however, especially through a telephone conversation. Operators have considerable latitude in deciding to grant service access according to seriousness of need.

Interpreting and Coding Service Requests

Police operators generally act with more discretion in performing their second gatekeeping task, interpreting and coding service demands. Requests for police service are initially articulated by callers in their terminology, from their point of view, and with their expectations about police response. Call takers must first make sense of the situation as reported, not always an easy task. "Citizens who are emotionally strained are not always models of clarity, concision, or coherence; the information they communicate may be sketchy or ambiguous" (Antunes and Scott, 1981: 166). Some service requests are so convoluted that it is almost impossible to understand the nature of the problem. Gatekeepers often probe to clarify demand messages and to obtain other relevant details about the demand situation. Few departments have established either basic or in-service training programs to teach effective means of probing for relevant information. Generally, call takers learn ways to gather this information through experience and peer observation.

Once demand information has been gathered and interpreted, it must be coded before a police unit can respond. Coding is the reformulation of demand information into agency-relevant terminology. The coding schemes used in most police departments partition all possible problems, no matter how complex, into finite, usually short, sets of numerical codes. These complaint or incident codes are used to represent the nature of the problem. They are often legalistic, crime-oriented schemes developed from extant penal codes. While they include categories for noncriminal services and assistance, these are usually outweighed by codes related to specific types of crime.

Many departments have also developed much shorter sets of codes to characterize the priority of service requests. Operators prioritize calls on the basis of seriousness and urgency. Although prioritization schemes vary, most departments have some means of identifying emergency calls such as a robbery in progress. Some systems also identify service requests to which rapid police response is unnecessary. These routine, nonemergency requests include reports of burglaries that happened several days previously or thefts where the caller only wants a police report for insurance purposes. The remainder of incoming calls are usually assigned an intermediate priority ranking.

Coding diverse demand and response information is necessary to process service requests efficiently. Without a shorthand description of the problem, police would be mired in a sea of verbiage, unable to respond quickly. Inherent in the coding process, however, is a reduction in information, a net loss, a potential distortion, all of which can influence the meaning of the information being coded. Each complaint code, unless it is very specific, can subsume numerous totally different situations. For example, the report of kids making noise might be classified as a disturbance, juvenile problem, argument, noise problem, curfew violation, or gang fight.

The exercise of discretion is fundamental to coding demand and response information. Police call takers are faced with information that is frequently ambiguous; they have little besides intuition to tell them whether the information reported by the caller is true or accurate. Because of the uncertainty involved, there will always be discretion in determining how to code any given request for service. Pepinsky's (1975:23) statement on patrol officer decision making is equally applicable to call takers: "The exercise of police discretion is fundamentally a matter of deciding how to treat ambiguous information." Police operators normally have more than one coding category to which they can assign a particular call. Their decisions can have significant consequences for both the police and the public.

Selection of Initial Response Alternative

A third task performed by call takers is the initial selection of police response. There are several alternative means of handling calls available to the operator; they are functions of service domain, organizational rules, and prevailing technology. In addition to promising to send a police unit to the scene, operators might transfer a caller to a report writer or other internal police unit, make a referral to another agency, provide relevant information, or simply refuse the request. Obviously, the nature and seriousness of the demand are primary influences on the selection of response alternatives. If a caller reports a serious problem, such as a bank robbery in progress, there is little doubt that several patrol units will be immediately sent to the scene. But for many demands, the nature of the problem and its urgency are not clear. The varied and complex nature of service demands often precludes developing rigid sets of rules for formulating responses applicable to all situations. Operator discretion in selecting responses is therefore prevalent where guidelines are nonexistent, vague, or unenforced. Where discretion is present, operator decisions may be affected by several factors, including the credibility of the caller, the mood of the operator, the current workload of either call takers or the patrol force, and the availability of other relevant resources.

Provision of Information to Service Seekers

A final gatekeeping task performed by police call takers is provision of information to persons requesting service. This information may take several forms, but is usually related to demand processing procedures or organizational response. Operators have considerable discretion in the manner in which they dispense information. Many times they participate in the demand articulation process, both by asking clarifying questions and by providing information about the department or other agencies and the services they render. For example, if a caller requests that the police perform a service that is outside their service domain, the operator may indicate that assistance can be obtained from another source and refer the caller to it. By asking probing questions, operators can help callers formulate a request that can be handled by the police.

Provision of information about police demand processing can influence citizen attitudes about and behavior toward service organizations. Callers may have little information concerning police processing of service requests, and as a result may be confused, unsettled, or angered by the procedures used to gather demand data. For example, callers faced with serious problems may be upset that operators interrupt and ask so many questions about the incident before promising to send a unit. They do not understand that information is routinely gathered to assist responding patrol units. Failure to provide some explanation of call-processing procedures may increase caller apprehension and diminish cooperation. There are few guidelines on the provision of information about police procedures, and operators therefore have widespread discretion in this area.

Through information provision operators not only affect service requests that may result in police response, but also can provide answers and solve many caller problems themselves. The importance and volume of information requests in which no police unit is needed have been largely overlooked in studies of demand patterns. Those few research efforts that have examined information calls indicate that they represent a significant segment of overall demand, and hence a large proportion of operator workload (Scott, 1981; Lilly, 1978). The types and extent of information provided are primary sources of operator discretion.

DISCRETION IN POLICE
RESPONSE COORDINATION

Gatekeeping is only one function in demand processing; the second is response coordination. The primary purpose of response coordination is to determine the specific dimensions of organizational response and to coordinate the efforts of service workers. In police departments the response coordination function is performed by dispatchers. In most large departments, persons answering telephone calls for service are distinct from persons dispatching field units. In smaller agencies the same person may perform both functions. While the following discussion presupposes functional separation, all departments perform both gatekeeping and response coordination tasks.

Dispatchers review calls for service information and dispatch appropriate units. They link callers with field officers who can respond, and also link officers to sources of information and support, both within and outside the department. Dispatchers, regardless of rank or status, generally act with the voice of the chief, and their instructions are so recognized. Wilson and McLaren (1972: 120) describe this function as the "giving of orders by an agent who has no authority in his own right, but who performs the routine tasks of command as a service for his principal." We have already described how police operators, as gatekeepers, have significant discretion in determining eligibility, assigning complaint codes, and providing information to callers. The middlepersons in the response process, the dispatchers, also maintain considerable discretion in determining the nature and specific components of police response.

Determining Specifics of Police Response

When the volume of calls for service exceeds response capacity, service queues form and responses must be sequenced. In these frequent situations the dispatcher must decide the order in which queued demands are to be serviced. The priority designations assigned by call takers cue dispatchers about sequencing responses; obviously, emergency calls receive immediate response from available units. At the other extreme, call takers usually assign low priority to routine, nonemergency calls to which rapid response is unnecessary, such as reports of "cold" burglaries or abandoned property. Dispatcher discretion is greatest for intermediate priority calls, which represent the most numerous type of demand and reflect a wide variety of crime, traffic, and assistance situations. Here relatively rapid police response is appropriate, although no immediate emergency is involved. Generally, police would like to respond to these calls within 10-15 minutes of their receipt. Sequencing responses to these calls is usually determined by dispatchers on the basis of further informal prioritization. Dispatchers must ascertain which calls with intermediate priority require more rapid response and which might safely remain a few more minutes in the queue. Of course, selection of calls to be dispatched may also be affected by patrol unit availability.

Determining police response to service requests also involves dispatcher decisions about which unit or units to send to the scene. Dispatchers in many departments have the undisputed right to assign jobs.[2] Their assignments are rarely refused, although they have little control over officer actions once a call is assigned. Dispatchers have some discretion in assigning units. Sending the nearest available unit is the usual decision rule, although other criteria may be used. Dispatchers may feel that in certain situations a specialized unit (such as a family crisis team or juvenile officer) or a patrol supervisor would be more appropriately sent than the nearest patrol unit. Alternatively, they may believe that a particular officer would be more effective than others in handling certain situations such as a rape investigation. Dispatchers also have latitude about the number of units to send and the designation of particular units as primary or backup.

Transmission of Service Request Information

A second response coordination task of dispatchers is transmitting information about both the demand situation and organizational response to officers in the field. Dispatchers may also indicate whether backup or other support units are being sent. Police dispatchers have little discretion in reporting complaint codes to officers; they simply read the codes as received from call takers (Pepinsky, 1976). Similarly, they report street address information as recorded by operators.

Dispatchers have greater discretion in deciding what other kinds of information about the service request to forward to responding officers. Often operators provide dispatchers with information about the demand in addition to a complaint code or street address (items required for police response). Included may be information about the participants or whether weapons or injuries are present. Dispatchers vary in the extent to which they broadcast this additional information.

Dispatcher dissemination of information to responding officers is an area in which divergent points of view on the role of broadcast information are clearly delineated. Some police officers and administrators believe that the more information of apparent relevance that can be provided to officers prior to their arrival at the scene, the better prepared they will be. Dispatchers sharing this perspective transmit most of the information forwarded by call takers. Others subscribe to Rubinstein's discussion of dispatch procedures in Philadelphia, where minimal information was provided to responding officers. In explaining why officers were not told about the exact nature of the complaint and were instead given only coded signals, Rubinstein (1973: 92) states:

> The dispatcher has no way of knowing whether he has been told the truth and must leave that determination to the investigating officer. There is no purpose in mentioning the specific complaint since it will all be repeated by the complainant when the officer arrives at the scene. The signal is also used to give an officer an assignment that involves a complex personal tale that the dispatcher cannot recount over the air or was unable to understand in the initial telling. . . . He simply uses the most general terms available to him.

Some administrators disagree with Rubinstein, arguing that there are advantages to providing all or most of the information available about an incident to responding officers. Complainants may be unable to repeat information about the incident to responding officers; that is, a victim may be injured too seriously to recount the matter, or a third party may be reporting the incident from a location other than that to which the police must respond. Additionally, officers may be better able to prepare themselves for handling service requests if they are provided relevant information prior to arriving at the scene. Of course, officers can request additional information from dispatchers. On the other hand, Federal Communications Commission regulations and departmental policies call for brevity on the airwaves. Despite disagreement on this issue, it is apparent that how much data dispatchers communicate beyond the most fundamental demand information is very much subject to their discretion.

THE IMPACT OF DISCRETION
ON POLICE PERFORMANCE

That police operators and dispatchers exercise broad discretion in carrying out their multiple functions should by now be clear. However, despite the prevalence of widespread discretion in gatekeeping and response coordination functions, the effects of operator and dispatcher decisions on police performance continue to be overlooked. There are several ways their decisions affect the job tasks of patrol officers and the types and quality of police services rendered.

The Impact of Police Operator Actions

Call takers set the agenda for a large portion of departmental workload. They first determine which callers are eligible to receive police service. Whether based on agency rules and policies or on operator perceptions and biases, each person calling the police is subject to eligibility screening. Persons denied access must look elsewhere for resolution of their problems. How operators treat callers may make a lasting impression and affect citizen attitudes toward police and caller willingness to report problems in the future. By defining some calls as outside police service domain, operators can reduce patrol officer workload and free them for routine patrol or assignment to other calls. This is especially important in times of high service demand, when even response to serious incidents may be delayed because of the unavailability of field units.

Operator discretion in coding calls also has important consequences for both the speed of police response and the types of services rendered. The incident or complaint code assigned by the operator defines the incident for all personnel that subsequently handle it, including dispatchers and patrol officers. Operators may also be responsible for assigning priority ranking to the request. The incident and priority codes subsequently affect the sequencing and unit assignment tasks of dispatchers, and these decisions affect response speed and activities (Manning, 1977).

The following police case demonstrates the consequences of operator discretion in coding service requests. The case involved a 13-year-old girl who called the police to report that someone was breaking into her home.

> The girl reported that a neighborhood youth was trying to break into her house. She was babysitting for her mother and was alone at the time. [The operator] took the girl's name and number, determined that the youth was known to the girl, and told her he would dispatch a police officer to her home. [The operator] classified the call as a "34," a routine disturbance call not requiring immediate response. The call was put in the "queue" to be answered when a squad car became available. The girl's mother came home 40 minutes later to discover that her daughter had been slain.

> "We get a lot of such calls," said [the division chief]. "Usually it is a pretty routine matter of neighborhood kids pestering a babysitter. [The operator's] mistake was to assume that was the case and not to elicit more information" [Police Magazine, 1981: 4].

In this case, a dramatic indication of what can happen as the result of a coding error, blame was placed squarely on the operator's designation of the call as a juvenile disturbance rather than a break-in in progress, which would have brought a quicker police response. Discretionary coding decisions such as this one occur hundreds of times each day, and mistakes can be made. Usually the errors invoke less serious consequences, but they certainly affect the lives of citizens and the overall performance of police agencies.

While it is the responsibility of responding officers to determine the full nature of the situation and to act accordingly, how fast they arrive and how well prepared they are to handle the situation are significantly influenced by the information obtained and passed on by call takers. If operators fail to gather relevant information about participants, weapons, or injuries, for example, officers may be ill prepared to handle the incident on arrival. This critical information is generally gathered by operators in a discretionary context which is for the most part devoid of guidelines and directives.

Operator discretion in selecting and activating initial police response can also have significant impact on both the police and the public. For many types of calls there are several possible responses that operators can initiate, including referral to other agencies, transfer to internal police units, and direct provision of information to callers. These responses may satisfy callers *without* dispatching an officer and also may conserve resources and reduce patrol force workload.

There are instances in which discretionary decision making in response selection by call takers can have severe consequences for citizens and police. In a recent case in Indianapolis, a man called the police to report that his father had been severely beaten and was in serious condition in a hospital. When told that the victim could not speak following surgery, the operator directed the caller to contact the homicide branch when his father's condition had improved. Since the incident occurred on the first day of the long Christmas weekend, the son was told to contact homicide in four days. By the time homicide was notified, the victim had died and the police investigation was severely hampered because it lacked information only the victim could provide. "The four-day delay in beginning the investigation points to a problem in the communications branch in deciding which calls police should respond to," the police chief admitted. "We probably have a policy problem there" (Indianapolis Star, December 31, 1981: 16). Even with a clear-cut policy, however, the operator's discretion in determining the mode of response remains a significant factor.

Operator discretion in providing information to service seekers is another important means of influencing the mode of service delivery. Many times callers want help with a particular problem, but have no idea where to turn; they call the police. Sometimes their problems are police matters, sometimes they are better handled by other agencies. Operators possess a tremendous amount of information about service delivery. Providing information to callers represents direct service delivery by operators. Additionally, they may create goodwill for the department in the same manner as an officer who is polite and helpful during encounters with citizens.

The Impact of Dispatcher Actions

Discretionary work activities of dispatchers also affect performance by influencing the speed and nature of police response to calls for service. Dispatchers have substantial latitude in the information they provide to responding officers beyond the minimal data about street address and complaint code. In some cases minimal information is sufficient, while in others additional information may help the officer prepare for the incident in advance and make quick sense of it on arrival. The extent and types of information the dispatcher forwards can influence what subsequently transpires in citizen-officer interactions.

An even greater source of dispatcher discretion stems from sequencing police responses to calls for service. By informal prioritization of calls and responses, dispatchers influence which incidents are handled quickly and which must wait for police action. The overall speed of police response, which is affected by dispatcher sequencing decisions, has been shown to affect outcomes such as arrest, location of witnesses, and citizen satisfaction with police (Percy, 1980; Kansas City Police Department, 1977; Pate et al. 1976; Parks, 1976). Call prioritization and response sequencing are necessitated by high demand volume relative to constrained police resources. Discretionary dispatcher decisions have crucial impact on subsequent police actions and public reactions.

Dispatchers' selection of responding units can also affect police activities and performance. Although the general decision rule is to dispatch the nearest available patrol unit, dispatchers may send detectives, technicians, crisis intervention teams, or other specialized units to the scene, depending on description of the incident. Dispatchers also decide whether to send backup units on a call, although officers sometimes "drive by" an incident location on their own. These choices, as with other dispatcher decisions, influence the amount and skills of the manpower assigned to service requests and therefore the activities and outcomes of police responses.

CONCLUSION AND POLICY IMPLICATIONS

Our purpose has been to point out the widespread existence of discretion in police gatekeeping and response coordination functions, and to elucidate ways in which discretion can affect police performance. Despite their far-reaching discretion, police telephone operators and dispatchers have been studied infrequently. Given the magnitude of the potential impact of discretion on police performance, it would seem appropriate for analysts, researchers, and administrators to focus more attention on discretion in the process of handling citizen calls for service.

Certainly one key policy issue facing administrators in the coming decade is the role of demand processing in policing. Will gatekeeping and response coordination continue to be viewed merely as internal support functions, or will they take their rightful place as service providing, performance affecting components of police response? There seems little doubt that as administrators search for answers to problems of increasing demand and diminishing resources, they will turn to nonpatrol modes of response such as referral or telephone report taking, which rely on call takers as primary response agents with discretionary decision-making power.

If so, it will be necessary to upgrade the status of police call takers and dispatchers. Demand-processing personnel must be more carefully selected, trained, supervised, and evaluated. Police gatekeepers and response coordinators have traditionally been poorly paid and undertrained. The complaint room of many police departments has become the repository of "the lame, the halt, and the blind." Departments have often assigned disabled or disciplined police officers to the sensitive tasks of answering calls or dispatching cars. Even persons assigned full-time to demand processing duties are frequently thrown into the breach with insufficient interpersonal communications skills and with no training in making crucial decisions in the pressure situations that frequently arise at police switchboards and dispatch consoles.

To handle the demand load more efficiently, police agencies must begin to hire and train call takers and dispatchers who can properly represent the department as service-providing agents. Recruitment programs, training schedules, and supervisory techniques must be developed and honed. More difficult, however, will be devising methods of evaluating the work of operators and dispatchers. The "horror stories" reported earlier are the most clear-cut manifestation of demand processing mistakes. Routine evaluation is much more difficult. How does one measure, for example, the soundness of call taker exercise of discretion? Some departments have relied on statistics such as the number of calls handled per shift. This is similar to evaluating patrol activity by counting officer arrests or numbers of tickets written. This measure reveals nothing about the accuracy of the call taker's rendering of the reported problem, the suitability of the response selected, or the eventual satisfaction of the caller.

One department with which we are familiar has adopted a procedure of taping, by voice-activated recorder, an entire shift of calls handled by each operator and dispatcher. Eight hours are thus reduced to only that portion of time in which the gatekeeper or response coordinator was busy. A sergeant then reviews each call, using a checklist to note such factors as how long it took to handle the call, whether the caller was asked to repeat information volunteered previously, whether the call taker was unnecessarily verbose, and the nature of the police response promised. Individuals being evaluated are then called in to discuss their performance. Supervisors highlight what they did correctly and point out areas in which improvement is necessary. This type of approach is promising in that it can potentially lead to awareness of the importance of individual technique, emphasize the exercise of call taker discretion, and improve police performance.

Another problem facing departments attempting to upgrade their call-processing procedures is development of incentive systems to ensure compliance with stated policies and goals: Can the evaluation system be supported through a series of rewards and sanctions? Many departments are governed by civil service regulations for promotion. Nevertheless, in some agencies supervisors reward "good" call takers by removing them from emergency phones and assigning them to quieter, nonemergency tasks. Consequently, the toughest jobs become the domain of the least competent personnel. Administrators face a difficult task in developing incentive systems for exemplary demand-processing behavior that do not ultimately harm agency performance.

More broadly, however, it is appropriate for the police to evaluate current discretionary practices to determine whether they yield positive or negative effects for both the department and the public. As Davis (1969: 25) convincingly argues, discretion is positive to the extent that it allows creative solutions to complex human problems, but it can also generate negative consequences when improperly used.

> Discretion is a tool, indispensable for individualization of justice. All governments in history have been governments of laws and of men. Rules alone, untempered by discretion, cannot cope with the complexities of modern government and of modern justice. Discretion is our principal source of creativeness in government and in law.

> Yet every truth extolling discretion may be matched by a truth about its dangers: Discretion is a tool only when properly used; like an axe, it can be a weapon for mayhem or murder. In a government of men and of laws, the portion that is a government of men, like a malignant cancer, often tends to stifle the portion that is a government of laws.

Discretion is both to be cherished and feared. Efforts further to analyze discretionary practices and their consequences, in both police and other public agencies, should provide information relevant to limiting and structuring discretion where it generates more bad than good. The optimal position is to have sufficient discretion to permit creative solutions while at the same time having sufficient limits to prevent harmful abuses.

NOTES

1. The widespread use of 911 systems since the late 1960s has further increased police-citizen telephone interaction, if not encounters. An easy-to-remember and widely publicized telephone number has made it simpler for citizens to contact police not only with reports of crimes and emergencies but with information requests and other nonessential calls.

2. In some agencies, field supervisors have authority to overrule dispatchers by ordering response delays or by directing other police units to respond to calls. Patrol supervisors are more likely to intervene when few units are available (that is, during times of high demand) and when intermediate or low-priority calls are concerned.

REFERENCES

ABERNATHY, G. M. (1962) "Police discretion and equal protection." South Carolina Law Quarterly 14: 472-486.

ANTUNES, G. and E. J. SCOTT (1981) "Calling the cops: police telephone operators and citizen calls for service." Journal of Criminal Justice 9: 165-180.

BLACK, D. J. (1970) "Production of crime rates." American Sociological Review 35: 733-748.

DAVIS, K. C. (1969) Discretionary Justice: A Preliminary Inquiry. Baton Rouge: Louisiana University Press.

GOLDSTEIN, H. (1977) Policing a Free Society. Cambridge, MA: Ballinger.

GOLDSTEIN, J. (1960) "Police discretion not to invoke the criminal process: low visibility decisions in the administration of justice." Yale Law Review 69: 543-594.

Indianapolis Star (1981) "Police dispatcher bungled call about beating, chief says." December 31, p. 16.

KADISH, S. H. (1962) "Legal norms and discretion in the police and sentencing processes." Harvard Law Review 75: 904-931.

Kansas City Police Department (1977) Response Time Analysis: Executive Summary and Volume II: Analysis Report. Kansas City, MO: Board of Police Commissioners.

LaFAVE, W. R. (1962a) "The police and non-enforcement of the law—part I." Wisconsin Law Review (January): 104-137.

——— (1962b) "The police and non-enforcement of the law—part II." Wisconsin Law Review (March): 177-239.

LILLY, J. R. (1978) "What are the police now doing?" Journal of Police Science and Administration 6: 51-60.

LIPSKY, M. (1980) Street Level Bureaucracy: Dilemmas of the Individual in Public Services. New York: Russell Sage.

MANNING, P. K. (1977) Police Work: The Social Organization of Policing. Cambridge, MA: MIT Press.

PARNAS, R. (1971) "Police discretion and diversion of incidents of intra-family violence." Law and Contemporary Problems 36: 539-565.

PATE, T., A. FERRARA, R. A. BOWERS, and J. LORENCE (1976) Police Response Time: Its Determinants and Effects. Washington, DC: Police Foundation.

PARKS, R. B. (1976) "Police response to victimization: citizen attitudes and perceptions," in W. G. Skogan (ed.) Sample Surveys of the Victims of Crime. Cambridge, MA: Ballinger.

PEPINSKY, H. E. (1975) "Police decision-making," in D. M. Gottfredson (ed.) Decision-Making in the Criminal Justice System. Washington, DC: National Institute of Mental Health.

——— (1976) "Police patrolmen's offense-reporting behavior." Journal of Research in Crime and Delinquency 13: 33-47.

PERCY, S. L. (1980) "Response time and citizen evaluation of police." Journal of Police Science and Administration 8: 75-86.

Police Magazine (1981) "A question of judgment." January, p. 4.

REISS, A. J., Jr. (1971) The Police and the Public. New Haven, CT: Yale University Press.

RUBINSTEIN, J. (1973) City Police. New York: Ballantine.

SCOTT, E. J. (1981) Calls for Service: Citizen Demand and Initial Police Response. Washington, DC: National Institute of Justice.

SILBERMAN, C. E. (1978) Criminal Violence, Criminal Justice. New York: Random House.

WILSON, J. Q. (1968) Varieties of Police Behavior. Cambridge, MA: Harvard University Press.

WILSON, O. W. and R. C. McLAREN (1972) Police Administration (3rd ed.). New York: McGraw-Hill.

7.

THE SOONER THE BETTER:
Some Effects of Police Response Time

Gary W. Cordner
University of Baltimore

Jack R. Greene

Tim S. Bynum
Michigan State University

For most of this century, a principal objective in police administration has been to minimize police officer response time to calls for service. It has been assumed that the sooner the police got to the scene of a crime or other problem, the better. The invention of motor cars and of mobile wireless radios, and their utilization by the police, enabled significant reductions in response time. Later innovations, such as patrol allocation models, optimal beat design techniques, and computer-aided dispatch systems, contributed to further minimization of police response time. The employment of such technology has been taken as an indication of the sophistication or "professionalism" of a police agency, and average response time is now commonly used as a police productivity measure.

Recent research, however, has cast considerable doubt on the importance of the presumed advantages accruing from reductions in response

Authors' Note: *Data collection and analysis for this study were supported in part by funds provided by the City of Pontiac, Michigan, for the evaluation of LEAA Grants 76-DF-05-0030, 77-DF-05-0012, and 78-DF-AX-0135. Dave Braunschneider, Steve Edwards, Dennis Lund, and Paul Rock assisted in the project evaluations. The preparation of this chapter was further aided by Bob Chandler.*

time. Basically, these studies have found that citizens rarely notify the police immediately on discovering crimes or other emergencies. For a variety of reasons, victims and witnesses often wait many minutes or even hours before calling the police. When the police receive the call, then, the incident is frequently quite old. Not surprisingly, therefore, it matters little whether the police take three, five, or ten minutes to get to the scene. Reducing the police component of response time by one or even a few minutes does not lead to much better outcomes when "citizen response time" is so lengthy to begin with.

Police emphasis on reducing reponse time has also had an unanticipated consequence for public relations. Public expectations of the speed at which the police should respond to calls for service have been altered and citizen tolerance for response time delay reduced. Citizen satisfaction with police services has been found to be associated with individual expectations of response time (Pate et al., 1976), irrespective of the kind or quality of police service provided. Simply put, citizens expect a quicker police response than they used to, and their evaluations of police performance are greatly shaped by whether or not the police arrive as soon as expected.

The analysis reported in this chapter examines the relationship between police response time and such outputs as on-scene arrests, witness availability, and final case status. The methods of analysis and some of the measures set this study apart from other recent response time research. The findings, though, are reasonably consistent with those of other studies. Generally, it is true that the sooner the police arrive, the better. But the capacity of the police to reach the scene very soon after the actual occurrence of a crime is severely limited, and the overall relationships between response time and desired outputs are weak.

PREVIOUS RESPONSE TIME RESEARCH

The first empirical analysis of response time effects was done for the President's Crime Commission by Herbert Isaacs (1967). He used dispatch records from Los Angeles to see whether faster police response led to more arrests and found a moderate relationship. His analysis also suggested that relatively small response time improvements (one minute) could result in substantial arrest increases when response time was already rapid (one to three or four minutes), but that such minor improvements would have negligible impact when response time was lengthy. The Isaacs study was widely citied for over a decade to help justify police utilization of technological innovations designed to minimize response time to crimes and emergencies.

An important limitation of the Isaacs study was that the response time-arrest relationship was based on analysis of only 70 cases. Two more recent studies from Seattle, also using dispatch records, employed larger samples. Clawson and Chang (1977) examined 2,532 calls, and their findings were very similar to those of Isaacs. Their results similarly suggested that small improvements in lengthy response times help very little, whereas shortening response time from four to three or from three to two minutes measurably enhances the probability of arrest. They also looked at two separate components of the police response interval, dispatch time and travel time, and found that neither was as strongly associated with arrest likelihood as was overall police response time.

In a replication and extension of the Clawson and Chang study, Tarr (1978) analyzed 3,639 calls handled by the Seattle Police Department. His findings were very consistent with those of the earlier studies. He was also able to decompose police response time into quarter-minute and half-minute segments, which allowed him to examine the effects of very small response time differences. He found even stronger relationships than had others between response time and arrests probability at the short end of the response time scale. The portions of calls resulting in arrests dropped dramatically for each fifteen-second increment for the first minute and one-half of response time, more gradually until the three- or four-minute mark, and then nearly leveled off.

These three dispatch records studies consistently point to a moderate relationship between response time and arrests, but they are beset by some serious shortcomings (Bertram and Vargo, 1976; Spelman and Brown, 1981).

(1) No distinctions were made between response-related arrests and other arrests.

(2) Dispatch records rely on officer self-reporting of arrival time at the scene. But officers will often report arrival while still en route (to avoid delay when they arrive). On other occasions, officers may not report arrival until well after they are at the scene (they may simply forget or not have time to waste).

(3) These studies were inherently correlational, and thus do not demonstrate cause and effect. Officers may respond faster when they sense that an arrest is probable, so that response time could be the dependent variable rather than arrest likelihood.

(4) No other consequences of response time but arrest were examined.
(5) Only the police components of response time (dispatch time and travel time) were measured.

Two major recent studies have addressed the foregoing problems. The Kansas City Police Department's (1978) *Response Time Analysis* distinguished between response-related and other arrests; used observers to independently verify police arrival time; looked at witness availability, injury, and citizen satisfaction as well as arrests; and conducted interviews to determine the magnitude of citizen delays in reporting crimes to the police. An important distinction was also made in the Kansas City study between discovery crimes (discovered only after their completion) and involvement crimes (detected by someone as the crime was taking place).

Taking these additional factors into consideration led to less sweeping conclusions about the importance of police response time. Median citizen reporting time for all Part I crimes was over six minutes, a not inconsiderable delay before police response could begin. As would be expected, citizen reporting time for involvement crimes was shorter than for discovery crimes. Arrests were made for almost 30 percent of involvement crimes, but for only 1 percent of citizen discovered crimes. When only response-related arrests were considered, however, the arrest rates for involvement and discovery crimes dropped to 7.7 and 0.2 percent, respectively. Overall, response-related arrests were made for only 3.7 percent of all Part I crimes.

The Kansas City study still found that the sooner the police arrive, the better. When both citizen reporting time and police response time were short, the probability of response-related arrest was higher, at least for involvement crimes. When reporting time exceeded ten minutes, though, police response time hardly mattered, even for involvement crimes. Within the category of involvement crimes, it was found that rapid response had greater effects for nonviolent than for violent cases. In violent involvement crimes, the perpetrator knew that the victim was immediately aware of the offense and so hastened escape. Also, in violent crimes the victim may be readily able to identify or even locate the assailant, so that rapid police response is less crucial for arrest probability. With nonviolent involvement crimes, however, it is more likely that the burglar or thief is unaware of the victim or witness observation and thus more likely still to be at the scene if the police are rapidly called and rapidly respond.

The relationships for witness availability were weak, but generally, the shorter the citizen reporting and police response times, the greater the probability that a witness other than the victim will be located for involvement crimes. Citizen reporting time was found to be unrelated to injury severity, but the police responded more rapidly the more serious the injury. The relationship between response time and citizen satisfaction was found to depend on citizen expectations. Police response time shorter than the citizen expected led to more satisfaction than response time in excess of expectations. This finding regarding the key role of citizen expectations in response time satisfaction is consistent with the results of other studies (Pate et al., 1976; Tien et al., 1977).

A second, recent study replicated and extended the Kansas City analysis in Peoria, Illinois, Jacksonville, Florida, San Diego, California, and Rochester, New York (Spelman and Brown, 1981). This study, sponsored by the Police Executive Research Forum (PERF), used extensive interviews of victims, witnesses, and bystanders in 3,300 serious crimes but did not use observers as had been done in Kansas City. Despite the somewhat different methodology, the authors reported that their findings unequivocally support those from the Kansas City analysis. Their strong conclusions include the following:

> Rapid police response may be unnecessary for three out of every four serious crimes reported to the police. The traditional practice of immediate response to all reports of serious crimes currently leads to on-scene arrests in only 29 of every 1,000 cases. By implementing innovative programs, police may be able to increase this response-related arrest rate to 50 or even 60 per 1,000, but there is little hope that further increases can be generated [Spelman and Brown, 1981: xix].

The PERF study found that median citizen delay in reporting involvement crimes ranged from four to five and one-half minutes and was about ten minutes for discovery crimes. Involvement crimes reported in progress had a response-related arrest probability of 35 percent; those reported within a few seconds, 18 percent; those reported one minute after the fact, 10 percent; and those reported within one and five minutes, 7 percent. Involvement crimes for which citizen reporting was delayed beyond five minutes had extremely low response-related arrest likelihoods. Of course, response-related arrest probabilities for discovery crimes were even lower. In sum, "police response time had no effect on the chances of on-scene arrest in 70 to 85 percent of Part I crimes because they were discovered after they had occurred, and had no effect on 50 percent to 80 percent of the rest because they were reported too slowly" (Spelman and Brown, 1981: 72). Therefore, "between 88 and 90 percent of serious crimes reported to the police were reported too slowly for a response-related arrest to be made, even if the police response time was zero" (Spelman and Brown, 1981: 74).

While substantially refining our understanding of the nature of response time, the importance of citizen reporting delays, and the relationship of these to arrests and other outcomes, the Kansas City and PERF studies are not without their limitations. An important limitation in both studies was that neither attempted to measure what might be termed "true response time." Both studies added the citizen reporting increment to the traditional dispatch time and travel time measures but ignored the elapsed time following the actual *occurrence* of the crime. This is particularly problematic in the consideration of discovery crimes. Discovery crimes follow a particular pattern: occurrence, discovery, reporting, dispatch, and arrival. Cumulatively, the period of time from occurrence to arrival represents true response time. But none of the studies reviewed here attempted to measure or analyze the importance of the time between occurrence and discovery, although one estimate is that 70 percent of offenses are reported ten or more minutes after occurrence (Elliott, 1973). In the research presented later in this chapter, time of occurrence is estimated, and the effects of true response time are examined.

The importance of true response time cannot be overstated. Traditional studies of police productivity have pursued the question of response time from the organization's perspective. That is, these studies tend to examine police response time as the portion of time falling under the control of the police agency. The time between dispatch and arrival and between receipt of a call from a citizen and dispatch have been of principal concern. Acknowledging that the citizen exercises discretion in calling the police for assistance (discovering to reporting) has tended to shift some of the responsibility for response time to citizens. From a policy standpoint this has resulted in efforts to encourage swifter citizen reporting of crime. But such efforts still ignore the time between occurrence and discovery of crime, a time interval that potentially overshadows the time involved in discovery-reporting-dispatch-arrival. The current inquiry attempts to shed some light on the independent effects of such elapsed time.

Despite their limitations, recent response time studies are already having a major impact on police thinking and policymaking. While just a few years ago "everyone knew" that minimizing police response time was highly desirable, it is fast becoming the conventional wisdom that "response time doesn't matter." This newer view exaggerates the findings and implications of the research, however. Response time does matter, albeit for only a portion of all crimes. It is still true that the sooner the police arrive, the better, but we now have a better appreciation of the nature of response time and impediments to reducing it.

RESEARCH SETTING

The data for this study come from the official records of the Pontiac, Michigan, Police Department and were part of a larger evaluation of its Integrated Criminal Apprehension Program (Grassie and Crowe, 1978; Cordner, 1979). Pontiac is a medium-sized, industrial community with a population of approximately 85,000, located 30 miles north of Detroit. It is much more of a center-city in its own right than a suburb, despite its location within the Detroit SMSA. It is the home of the Pontiac Motor Division, General Motors Truck and Coach, and several other major manufacturing concerns. Quite a large number of people work in Pontiac but live in the more rural and suburban areas of Oakland County (which has about one million residents). The reported index crime rate for the city is about twice that for the nation as a whole and is also well above the average for other cities in the same size category.

Two sets of data were analyzed. The first analysis uses monthly data for the period January 1975 to September 1979 (57 months) to estimate the effects of average police response time and several other variables on the monthly number of on-scene arrests. This analysis closely approximates the traditional approach to examining the effects of response time. The second analysis focuses on 1,688 incidents occurring during five sample weeks between July 1978 and July 1979 to estimate true response time and its effects on arrests, witness availability, and several other output measures. The data and methods are further described in conjunction with the analyses that follow.

RESPONSE TIME AND ON-SCENE ARRESTS

Previous response time studies have used the case or incident as the unit of analysis, analyzing the relationships between case characteristics (response time) and case outcomes (arrests). As an alternative approach, the research reported in this section uses months as units of analysis. The dependent variables are (1) the monthly number of index crime on-scene arrests and (2) the monthly number of burglary on-scene arrests. The monthly total of index crime on-scene arrests in Pontiac during the 57-month period ranged from 31 to 89, while burglary on-scene arrests ranged from 4 to 17 per month.

The selection of total monthly index crime on-scene arrests and those for burglary as dependent variables was predicated on an observed relationship found between on-scene arrests and larceny. In Pontiac, and we suspect in other cities, when a retail security guard apprehended a suspect for shoplifting (larceny), the police would be called, they would respond and take the suspect into custody, and an on-scene arrest would be credited. These on-scene larceny arrests clearly have nothing to do with response time or other independent variables, such as competing calls for service or patrol deployment levels. Thus, total monthly index crime on-scene arrests are potentially distorted by on-scene larceny arrests. In addition, burglary as a crime type represented, in Pontiac, a significant proportion of all property crimes. Moreover, burglary tends to be a discovery crime where the time interval between occurrence and discovery can be quite lengthy. As a consequence of the potential bias introduced by the larceny on-scene arrests and given that burglary represents a major portion of property crimes, a separate analysis using burglary as a dependent variable was conducted.

The principal independent variable of interest is the monthly average primary call response time. This measures the average elapsed time, from receipt of call by the police department to arrival at the scene by a patrol unit, for calls involving serious crimes, crimes in progress, and emergencies (such as personal injury accidents). It is important to note that this average response time measure does not account for citizen reporting delays—it uses the traditional measure of police response time. Also, arrival times for computing the average were self-reported by responding patrol units and not independently verified by observers.

Other independent variables used were the average daily number of patrol units deployed each month, the monthly number of reported offenses, and the number of other kinds of calls per month. More units deployed might lead to more on-scene arrests, either by rapid response or by increased in-progress detection. More index crimes occurring might lead to more index crime on-scene arrests simply because of increased opportunities (the same would apply for burglaries and burglary on-scene arrests). On the other hand, more calls involving incidents other than index crimes might lead to fewer index crime on-scene arrests, because patrol units are busy doing other things (again, the same reasoning would apply for burglaries). Hernandez (1981a, 1981b) has reported more generally such an inverse relationship between call for service demand and proactive police activity.

The results of the analysis of monthly total index crime and burglary on-scene arrests are presented in Table 7.1. For both dependent variables, the coefficients for primary call response time and number of reported offenses are sizable. As predicted, shorter response times are associated with more on-scene arrests (− .30 and − .24 respectively), more reported index crimes with more index crime arrests (.27), and more burglaries with more burglary arrests (.28). The coefficients for patrol deployment levels and number of other kinds of calls are much smaller than the other independent variables and much less consistent. The overall R^2 values for both equations are rather small, and that for index crime is statistically significant, while the one for burglaries is not.

The consistent coefficients across both analyses for response time and number of offenses suggest that we can be reasonably confident about their apparent relationships with numbers of on-scene arrests. On-scene arrests, then, are positively related to the available pool of reported incidents while inversely related to response time. Given the data presented in Table 7.1, a tentative conclusion is that the sooner the police respond the better, irrespective of deployment levels or competing calls for service. Such a conclusion provides moderate support for the previous response time studies cited. But the issue of what actually constitutes true response time remains unresolved.

TRUE RESPONSE TIME

When patrol officers file incident reports in Pontiac, they are asked to indicate time of occurrence. Occasionally this is known precisely, but at other times it must be estimated. The victim may know that the offense occurred within, say, a two-hour period, or that it may have happened any time during the week that a family was on vacation. Commercial burglaries are commonly discovered on Monday mornings and therefore must have happened sometime since closing time on Friday. Barroom assaults are often reported the next day, with the victim sure only that it happened "sometime last night."

As part of data collection and analysis for the 1,688 incidents occurring during the five sample weeks in Pontiac, estimated time of occurrence was noted. Whenever the patrol officer specified in a report only a range of time, the midpoint was used as the estimated time of occurrence. While perhaps not a very accurate estimating procedure for any single incident, this method arguably approximates times of occurrence reasonably well over a large number of incidents.

"Most likely time occurred" for each incident was estimated as described above. The remaining time points were taken directly from incident reports completed by patrol officers, who in turn usually got them from dispatch records. It should be noted that "time reported" is actually the moment that the telephone operator time-stamps the call card; "time dispatched" is the moment the dispatcher time-stamps the

TABLE 7.1 Multiple Regression Analysis of Monthly Number of On-Scene Arrests for All Index Crimes and for Burglaries as Functions of Various Activity and Workload Measures (N = 57 months)

			Independent Variables[a]				
Dependent Variable	Average Daily Patrol Units Deployed	Number of Reported Index Crimes	Number of Reported Burglaries	Number of Calls Other Than Index Crimes	Number of Calls Other Than Burglaries	Primary Call Response Time	R^2
Monthly number of index crime on-scene arrests	-.14	.27		.15		-.30	3.95[b]	.27
Monthly number of burglary on-scene arrests	-.01		.28		-.02	-.24	1.67	.14

a. Coefficients presented are standardized.
b. Statistically significant at the .05 level.

card, presumably as a unit is assigned the call; "time arrived" is the moment the dispatcher time-stamps the card, presumably as the patrol unit reports its arrival, which presumably coincides with actual arrival; and "time completed" is the moment the dispatcher time-stamps the card, presumably as the patrol unit reports its completion of the call, which presumably coincides with actual completion. The problem with self-reported arrival time was noted earlier and pertains here. The rest of the foregoing "presumably" statements did not seem to have introduced any systematic bias in the data and are offered mainly to clarify the sources of response time information.

Using the estimate of occurrence together with the actual time intervals for time reported to time dispatched, dispatch to arrival, and arrival to completion enabled the calculation of a median time interval for each stage in response time. The resulting time intervals suggest that the interval between occurrence and reporting completely overshadows all other time considerations. In the Pontiac data, the median interval for time occurred to time reported was 201.5 minutes, while report to dispatch was 2.5 minutes, dispatch to arrival was 9.0 minutes, and arrival to call completion was 37.7 minutes. With such time intervals it is obvious that a tremendous amount of time passes before many incidents are reported to the police. Up to ten or twenty minutes of this time may be attributable to citizen reporting delay (as suggested in previous studies), but the remaining *three hours* must be time between occurrence and discovery. Dispatch time and travel time are minuscule for the median incident compared to time lost prior to citizen discovery and reporting.

Pursuing the issue of true response time the time components for several specific crime types are presented in Table 7.2. Median dispatch time is shortest for assaults and robbery and longest for burglary. Travel time is shortest for robbery and longest for malicious destruction. True response time (time of occurrence until time police arrive) is also shortest for robbery and assaults, and longest for larceny (with shoplifting excluded for reasons explained earlier). Incredibly, the median true response time for larceny is eight hours, and it is nearly five and one-half hours for burglary. Obviously, most of these offenses are discovery crimes, often discovered long after occurrence. The shorter median true response times are all for involvement crimes, although these also exceed one-half hour.

RESPONSE TIME EFFECTS BY CRIME TYPE

Using the same data set (1,688 incidents) from which true response time was estimated, one can investigate the relationships between response

TABLE 7.2   Median Response Time by Crime Type (in minutes)

Crime Type	N	Time Reported Until Time Dispatched	Time Dispatched Until Time Arrived	Time Arrived Until Time Completed	True Response Time: Estimated Time Occurred Until Time Arrived
All offenses	1674	2.5	9.0	37.7	213.0
Burglary	257	6.1	10.1	50.7	325.0
Robbery	44	2.8	4.2	77.0	32.5
Aggravated assault	93	1.0	7.2	47.7	35.5
Larceny*	378	5.5	9.9	30.2	483.5
Assault & battery	193	0.6	4.8	33.4	42.0
Malicious destruction	219	5.4	10.6	31.6	267.0

*Does not include larcenies from commercial buildings (mostly shoplifting) or larcenies from persons.

time and various case outputs. This follows the traditional form of response time research, with the case or incident as the unit of analysis. As with the early response time studies, this analysis has several serious limitations: Response-related arrests and other outcomes are not differentiated; patrol arrival time is self-reported; and relationships are merely correlational with no empirical evidence of causation available. But this study has several positive features too: Both the traditional measure and true response time are used; six specific crime types are examined, along with an overall offense category; and a variety of outputs and outcomes are investigated.

Traditional analyses of police response time have used on-scene arrests as the primary dependent variable. The use of the on-scene arrest variable is predicated on the assumption that quicker response will likely find the criminal suspect closer to the criminal act and will increase the likelihood of immediate arrest. As we have seen, though, there is often an extreme time interval between occurrence and reporting. Alternative police outputs can also be identified, however, that may not be as sensitive to the time delays as on-scene arrest may be. In this regard recent police productivity assessments have focused on investigative case screening, the expanded role of the patrol officer in conducting preliminary investigations, and the weighing of cases according to solvability factors (indicators of whether cases are likely to be cleared by arrest) as methods for improving police investigatory capacity (Bloch and Bell, 1976; Cawley et al., 1977; Greenberg et al., 1977; Greenwood et al., 1977; Eck, 1979). Improving and managing criminal investigations also includes a concern for patrol officer initial response to a crime scene. Such response by patrol might lead to the identification of witnesses, suspects, vehicles, and physical evidence that would be useful to future investigations and ultimately to case clearances through arrests. Rapid response, then, is thought to improve the potential for identifying witnesses, suspects, and evidence, thereby enhancing investigative outcomes.

Bivariate correlations between response times and four selected "solvability factors" are presented in Table 7.3. Correlations for each crime type are provided between the solvability factors and two measures of response time: traditional police response time (report to arrival or dispatch time plus travel time), and true response time (occurrence to arrival).

It is noteworthy that the vast majority of coefficients in Table 7.3 are negative, indicating that shorter response times are associated with higher probabilities of witness availability, suspect identification, suspect vehicle identification, and physical evidence availability. On the other hand, most of the coefficients are rather small, indicating that response time is not strongly related to these indicators of solvability. A fair proportion of the coefficients are statistically significant, but primarily due to large sample sizes rather than strong relationships.

Of the solvability factors, witness availability and suspect identification are most associated with response time. Suspect vehicle identification is only very weakly related to response time, while overall the availability of physical evidence seems unrelated to response time. Interestingly, though, shorter true response times for burglaries are associated with a weak but significantly greater likelihood that physical evidence will be located.

The relationships between response times and solvability factors differ somewhat by crime type. Response time, particularly true response time, seems to matter most for burglaries and least for robberies. Generalizing a bit further, response time seems to matter more for property crimes than for violent crimes. Several of the strongest relationships, however, are for traditional response time for assaultive crimes. These also provide the biggest differences between traditional and true response time coefficients. An exact explanation for this has not been discovered, but three partial reasons might be that (1) many assaults are reported the next day at the police station, for which traditional response time is recorded as zero, (2)

TABLE 7.3   Pearson Correlations Between Response Time Measures and Selected Solvability Factors by Crime Type

Crime Type and Response Measure	N	Was There A Witness?	Can Suspect Be Identified?	Can Suspect Vehicle Be Identified?	Is There Physical Evidence?
All offenses					
Report to arrival[a]	1642	–.14	–.13	–.06	–.01
Occur to arrival[b]	1631	–.19	–.12	–.05	–.01
Burglary					
Report to arrival	259	–.13	–.07	–.02	.01
Occur to arrival	256	–.20	–.12	–.02	–.12
Robbery					
Report to arrival	45	NV	.11	–.08	–.07
Occur to arrival	44	NV	.07	–.07	–.06
Aggravated assault					
Report to arrival	96	–.02	–.25	–.08	–.06
Occur to arrival	96	.06	.10	–.07	–.07
Larceny[c]					
Report to arrival	382	–.08	–.07	–.04	–.03
Occur to arrival	380	–.11	.04	–.02	–.06
Assault & battery					
Report to arrival	197	–.21	–.22	–.02	NV
Occur to arrival	196	.02	.04	–.05	NV
Malicious destruction					
Report to arrival	222	–.13	–.14	–.08	.06
Occur to arrival	221	–.14	–.04	–.06	–.03

NOTE: Coefficients underlined are statistically significant at the .05 level using a one-tailed test. NV = no variance (coefficient could not be computed).

a. Time reported to the police until time the police arrived.
b. Estimated time occurred until time the police arrived.
c. Does not include larcenies from commercial buildings (mostly shoplifting) or larcenies from persons.

assaults are most likely to involve a perpetrator known to the assailant, so that solvability depends little on true response time, and (3) traditional response time may be dependent on reported assault seriousness, and seriousness may be related to solvability (including victim preference for arrest), so that the relationship is inverse and spurious.

Bivariate correlations between response times and three measures of investigative effort are presented in Table 7.4. These variables are really neither outputs nor outcomes, but rather indicate whether subsequent investigative follow-up activity is associated with initial response time. Three such interim investigative processes were selected for analysis: whether or not an evidence technician was called to the scene of the incident, whether or not investigators conducted a follow-up investigation, and the extent of investigative follow-up devoted to the incident. Investigative follow-up was measured on an ordinal scale with three categories: (1) investigator reviews report only, (2) investigator makes a few phone calls to principals in the investigation, or (3) investigator conducts a more intensive investigation. Included in this latter category would be such investigative behaviors as visiting the crime scene, searching for additional evidence or witnesses, using informants, or conducting records checks.

Again, the important issue in examining these interim police processes is whether or not initial response time, including the time interval from estimated occurrence to reporting, is related to more police activity, whether or not such activity results in an arrest or clearance. Overall, the relationships are negligible, although again most of the coefficients are negative, indicating that more investigative follow-up effort is applied in cases with shorter response times.

Of particular interest are the strong negative relationships between traditional response time and initiation and extent of investigative follow-up for robbery and aggravated assault. The most likely explanation seems to be that the police respond rapidly to serious robberies and assaults and that seriousness is a predictor of investigative follow-up activity. Thus, again, response time could be a dependent rather than an independent variable, and its association with follow-up effort may be spurious as well. In a previous study using some of the same data, however, we found that for the general category of personal offenses, injury severity was not strongly related to extent of follow-up investigation (Bynum et al., forthcoming). Looking back at Table 7.4, though, it can be seen that the coefficients for assault and battery (a less serious personal offense) are positive. The explanation offered above may be valid, then, for the subcategories of robbery and aggravated assault, though not for all personal crimes as a single category.

Relationships between response time and three case outcome measures are presented in Table 7.5. As with the preceding two tables, the vast majority of the correlation coefficients are negative, indicating that shorter response times are associated with better case outcomes. The coefficients are all rather small, however, although quite a few are statistically significant.

It is interesting that final case status is consistently associated with traditional response time. Two explanations may pertain here: The police may respond faster when they have reason to believe that case clearance is likely; and, particularly for assaults, many cases reported at the police station (zero response time) are at least exceptionally cleared (perpetrator is known, though the victim may not desire prosecution). Of course, these post hoc explanations may not be valid, reasonable as they seem.

The crime type most consistently showing a relationship between response time and case outcome is burglary. This is consistent with the findings from previous studies about the importance of response time for nonviolent involvement offenses. The perpetrators of these kinds of crimes are less likely to know that they have been detected by a witness, and are generally in less of a hurry to escape, than are perpetrators of violent, personal offenses.

DISCUSSION

The desirability of minimizing police response time is based on assumptions about criminal behavior and evidence availability at crime scenes. Rapid response is believed to improve police capacity to intercept criminal suspects at or near the crime scene, particularly for involvement crimes. Improvements in police response time are also thought to improve the chances of locating witnesses and physical evidence, making subsequent clearance and/or arrest more likely, especially for discovery crimes.

Analysis of both data sets used in this study provides some support for the view that the sooner the police arrive, the better. More on-scene arrests, more evidence, more investigative effort, and better case outcomes tend to be associated with shorter police response time, although the relationships are not terribly strong and vary by crime type.

True response time, as compared to the period of time most likely to fall within the control of the police agency (the citizen reporting to police arrival increment), was found to be very lengthy. Median true response time for property crimes must be measured in hours, and is at least thirty minutes even for personal assaultive crimes. This "discovery delay," when

TABLE 7.4   Pearson Correlations Between Response Time Measures and Selected Investigative Activities Undertaken by Crime Type

Crime Type and Response Measure	N	Was Evidence Technician Work Performed?	Was There an Investigative Follow-up?	Extent of Investigative Follow-up
All offenses				
Report to arrival[a]	1686	−.02	−.04	−.03
Occur to arrival[b]	1674	−.07	−.03	−.01
Burglary				
Report to arrival	260	−.03	−.06	−.08
Occur to arrival	257	−.11	−.04	−.02
Robbery				
Report to arrival	45	−.05	−.35	−.27
Occur to arrival	44	−.04	.07	.14
Aggravated assault				
Report to arrival	96	−.06	−.31	−.28
Occur to arrival	96	−.03	−.11	−.07
Larceny[c]				
Report to arrival	382	−.06	−.03	−.06
Occur to arrival	380	−.07	−.05	.01
Assault & battery				
Report to arrival	198	NV	.10	.13
Occur to arrival	197	NV	.05	.13
Malicious destruction				
Report to arrival	223	−.02	−.02	.01
Occur to arrival	222	−.03	−.01	−.05

NOTE: Coefficients underlined are statistically significant at the .05 level using a one-tailed test. NV = no variance (coefficient could not be computed).

a. Time reported to the police until time the police arrived.
b. Estimated time occurred until time the police arrived.
c. Does not include larcenies from commercial buildings (mostly shoplifting) or larcenies from persons.

TABLE 7.5   Pearson Correlations Between Response Time Measures and Selected Case Outcomes by Crime Type

Crime Type and Response Measure	N	Were Arrests Made?	Final Case Status	Court Action
All offenses				
Report to arrival[a]	1672	−.05	−.14	−.06
Occur to arrival[b]	1660	−.11	−.12	−.09
Burglary				
Report to arrival	260	−.13	−.12	−.12
Occur to arrival	257	−.11	−.13	−.10
Robbery				
Report to arrival	44	−.08	−.08	−.08
Occur to arrival	43	−.08	−.10	−.07
Aggravated assault				
Report to arrival	96	−.07	−.24	−.04
Occur to arrival	96	.12	.11	.13
Larceny[c]				
Report to arrival	379	−.08	−.10	−.06
Occur to arrival	377	−.06	−.00	−.05
Assault & battery				
Report to arrival	194	−.02	−.13	−.06
Occur to arrival	193	−.08	.06	−.08
Malicious destruction				
Report to arrival	222	−.07	−.13	−.04
Occur to arrival	221	−.09	−.05	−.09

NOTE: Coefficients underlined are statistically significant at the .05 level using a one-tailed test.

a. Time reported to the police until time the police arrived.
b. Estimated time occurred until time the police arrived.
c. Does not include larcenies from commercial buildings (mostly shoplifting) or larcenies from persons.

added to the citizen reporting delay uncovered by previous studies, reinforces the view that rapid response by the police may not make sense for many, or perhaps most, offenses. It does not seem crucial for the police to rush to the scene of a crime that actually occurred hours before.

Still, when true response time is short, better outcomes are more likely. The principal policy implication of this and previous studies is the need for police agencies to develop differentiated responses to reported crimes. The police need to identify, from among the many calls that they receive, those that are hot or at least still warm. Response time to these kinds of calls should be minimized by the police. The remaining call for service workload can be managed by the police, using delayed response, report taking over the telephone, and other strategies.

Police telephone operators and dispatchers will never be able to distinguish exactly between calls that deserve a rapid response and ones that do not, of course, since they inevitably must work with incomplete and inaccurate information. We will probably always prefer that they err on the side of caution, opting for immediate response whenever it *might* seem necessary. Nevertheless, this and earlier studies clearly indicate that a large portion of calls can be readily identified as not needing rapid response and hence assigned for some other mode of handling.

The potential for greatest improvement in police response effectiveness lies in the reduction of true response time through reduction in the discovery delay. Some of the clearest ways of achieving this reduction, such as increased police and electronic surveillance, have obvious drawbacks, however. Other methods, such as increased use of alarms, are somewhat more benign. Target-hardening efforts that force the offender to make more noise or be more visible while committing the crime might enhance early discovery and reduce response delay. Community crime prevention efforts that encourage neighbors to report suspicious activity are also encouraging as a means of reducing true police response time. Finally, directed patrol strategies that deploy police in areas where they are most likely to detect crimes in progress, and that provide them with information about what to look for, are promising.

REFERENCES

BERTRAM, D. K. and A. VARGO (1976) "Response time analysis study: preliminary findings on robbery in Kansas City." Police Chief (May): 74-77.
BLOCH, P. B. and J. BELL (1976) Managing Investigations: The Rochester System. Washington, DC: Police Foundation.

BYNUM, T. S., G. W. CORDNER, and J. R. GREENE (forthcoming) "The impact of victim and offense characteristics on police investigative decision making." Criminology.

CAWLEY, D. F., H. J. MIRON, W. J. ARAUJO, R. WASSERMAN, T. A. MANNELLO, and Y. HUFFMAN (1977) Managing Criminal Investigations: Manual. Washington, DC: U.S. Department of Justice.

CLAWSON, C. and S. K. CHANG (1977) "The relationship of response delays and arrest rates." Journal of Police Science and Administration 5: 53-68.

CORDNER, G. W. (1979) The Pontiac Integrated Criminal Apprehension Project: A Final Evaluation Report. East Lansing: School of Criminal Justice, Michigan State University.

ECK, J. E. (1979) Managing Case Assignments: The Burglary Investigation Decision Model Replication. Washington, DC: Police Executive Research Forum.

ELLIOTT, J. F. (1973) Interception Patrol. Springfield, IL: Charles C Thomas.

GRASSIE, R. G. and T. D. CROWE (1978) Integrated Criminal Apprehension Program: Program Implementation Guide. Washington, DC: U.S. Department of Justice.

GREENBERG, B., C. V. ELLIOT, L. P. KRAFT, and H. S. PROCTER (1977) Felony Investigation Decision Model. Washington, DC: U.S. Department of Justice.

GREENWOOD, P. W., J. CHAIKEN, and J. PETERSILIA (1977) The Criminal Investigation Process. Lexington, MA: D. C. Heath.

HERNANDEZ, E., Jr. (1981a) "The influence of tight budgets on proactive law enforcement," in J. J. Fyfe (ed.) Contemporary Issues in Law Enforcement. Beverly Hills, CA: Sage.

——— (1981b) "Police calls for service, observation arrests and proactive law enforcement," presented at the Western Society of Criminology, Newport Beach, California.

ISAACS, H. H. (1967) "A study of communications, crimes, and arrests in a metropolitan police department," in Task Force Report: Science and Technology. Washington, DC: U.S. Department of Justice.

Kansas City Police Department (1978) Response Time Analysis: Executive Summary. Washington, DC: U.S. Department of Justice.

PATE, T., A. FERRARA, R. A. BOWERS, and J. LORENCE (1976) Police Response Time: Its Determinants and Effects. Washington, DC: Police Foundation.

SPELMAN, W. and D. K. BROWN (1981) Calling the Police: Citizen Reporting of Serious Crime. Washington, DC: Police Executive Research Forum.

TARR, D. P. (1978) "Analysis of response delays and arrest rates." Journal of Police Science and Administration 6: 429-451.

TIEN, J. M., J. W. SIMON, and R. C. LARSON (1977) An Alternative Approach in Police Patrol: The Wilmington Split-Force Experiment. Cambridge, MA: Public Systems Evaluation.

ABOUT THE AUTHORS

David N. Allen is Assistant Professor of Public Administration at Pennsylvania State University, University Park, Pennsylvania. He previously taught at the University of Louisville. He has published in the areas of police management, local energy policy, and municipal cable television regulation. Currently he is engaged in studies on police supervision and high-technology economic development.

Richard R. Bennett is Associate Professor in the School of Justice at The American University. He received his Ph.D. at Washington State University and has served on the faculties of the University of Michigan and Youngstown State University. He has also served as Director of Research for a state planning agency and as a criminal investigator in the field. He has published in the areas of police socialization, cognition, and behavior, as well as justice policy research. His current research and publications deal with cross-national theory construction and the comparative analysis of police effects on crime and crime clearance rates.

Tim S. Bynum received his Ph.D. in criminology from Florida State University and is currently Associate Professor in the School of Criminal Justice at Michigan State University. His recent publications include articles on the factors associated with the granting of pretrial release, racial disparity in parole decisions, and the police decision to investigate a criminal complaint. He is currently involved in a project investigating the use of secure detention for juvenile offenders.

Gary W. Cordner is Assistant Professor and Graduate Program Director in the Department of Criminal Justice at the University of Baltimore. His

Ph.D. in social science/criminal justice from Michigan State University was completed in 1980. He has published several articles on police-related subjects and has co-authored texts on police administration and criminal justice planning. He is currently engaged in a study of repeat offenders and an evaluation of police efforts to reduce fear of crime in Baltimore County, Maryland.

Alan S. Engel is Assistant Chair and Professor of Political Science at Miami University. He has published in the areas of criminal justice and constitutional rights and liberties. He has also served as a consultant to various police agencies.

David J. Giacopassi is Associate Professor in the Department of Criminal Justice at Memphis State University. He received his Ph.D. in sociology from the University of Notre Dame. His current research interests center on career contingencies and the adjustment of individuals within the police organization.

Jack R. Greene is Associate Professor in the School of Criminal Justice at Michigan State University. He has published in the areas of criminal justice and police decision making, police organization and administration, public policy, and the evaluation of police services. He has recently edited an anthology of papers on police management, *Managing Police Work: Issues and Analysis* (Sage, 1982) and is currently working on models of police careers.

Steven H. Hatting is Assistant Professor of Political Science at the College of St. Thomas (Minnesota). He specializes in the areas of criminal justice and constitutional law. He has an article forthcoming in the *Journal of Police Science and Administration.*

Stephen Mastrofski is Assistant Professor of Administration of Justice at The Pennsylvania State University, University Park. He received his Ph.D. in political science at the University of North Carolina. During his graduate studies, he was field research site director in Tampa-St. Petersburg, Florida, on a study of police organization and performance. He has conducted research on police organization and the evaluation of police performance.

Michael G. Maxfield is Assistant Professor of Public Affairs and Assistant Professor of Forensic Studies at Indiana University, Bloomington. He is co-author, with Wesley Skogan, of *Coping With Crime: Individual and Neighborhood Reactions,* and has published articles on police behavior in *Social Science Quarterly* and *Public Administration Review.* He is currently working on a study of police patrol supervision.

John P. McIver is a Research Associate at the Workshop in Political Theory and Policy Analysis at Indiana University. His research interests include analysis of public policy issues, American politics, and methodology. In addition to co-authoring *Unidemensional Scaling* (Sage, 1981), he had published research findings in the *American Journal of Political Science, American Politics Quarterly, Policy Studies Journal, Policy and Politics, Political Methodology,* and several edited collections.

Roger B. Parks is Associate Director of the Workshop in Political Theory and Policy Analysis and a Lecturer in the Department of Political Science at Indiana University. His publications include work on urban police departments, public administration, and research methods.

Stephen L. Percy is Assistant Professor of Government and Foreign Affairs at the University of Virginia. His chapter was written while he was a Research Associate at the Workshop in Political Theory and Policy Analysis at Indiana University. While there, he served as Study Director of a National Institute of Justice-funded study of citizens' demands and information flow associated with police response to calls for service. He has published articles in *Policy Studies Journal,* the *Journal of Police Science and Administration,* and *Public Productivity Review.*

Philip A. Russo, Jr., is Associate Professor of Political Science at Miami University, where he teaches and does research in the area of public administration. He has published articles in *Publius* and *Policy Perspectives.*

Eric J. Scott is a Research Associate at the Workshop in Political Theory and Policy Analysis at Indiana University. He has participated in and directed several research efforts involving police operations. He is currently Co-Principal Investigator of a study funded by the National Institute of

Justice to examine initial police response to citizen demands and information flow related to police demand processing. His publications have concentrated on citizen demand patterns, police communications, and police referral practices.

Jerry R. Sparger is Associate Professor in the Department of Criminal Justice at Memphis State University. He received his Ph.D. in psychology from the University of Tennessee. His current research focuses on psychological change in police recruits, job satisfaction and turnover in police agencies, and mid-life adjustment of lower-ranking personnel in police departments.